LENTEN

# *GOSPEL*

REFLECTIONS

BISHOP ROBERT BARRON

WITH REFLECTION QUESTIONS BY
PEGGY PANDALEON

WORD on FIRE.

Published by Word on Fire, Elk Grove Village, IL 60007

Cover design, typesetting, and interior art direction by
Rozann Lee, Cassie Bielak, and Katherine Spitler

ISBN: 978-1-68578-089-0

Library of Congress Control Number: 2023942721

# *INTRODUCTION*

Friends,

Thank you for joining me as we journey together toward the great feast of Easter!

Lent is a season for refocusing on the suffering and death of our Lord Jesus Christ, so that we will be ready to embrace the good news of the Resurrection.

Why this emphasis on suffering? Because Christ saved us through an act of suffering. He bore in his own person the weight of our sin and died for us on the cross, where suffering and love coincided.

And the Church is the Body of Christ, which participates in Christ. Therefore, we shouldn't be surprised that we will be called upon to suffer out of love. In the economy of grace, God may use our suffering to bear the burden of another member of the Body of Christ, just as one system can take up the work of another, or one organ can support another.

So as we begin with Ash Wednesday, let us resolve to focus on Christ's suffering, and to unite our own suffering—through fasting, prayer, almsgiving, and reflection on the Stations of the Cross—with the suffering members of the Church. It is not the destination but the journey that will ultimately transform us.

Peace,

+ Robert Barron

Bishop Robert Barron

LENTEN
# GOSPEL
REFLECTIONS

# FEBRUARY 14, 2024

### Ash Wednesday

### Matthew 6:1–6, 16–18

Jesus said to his disciples: "Take care not to perform righteous deeds in order that people may see them; otherwise, you will have no recompense from your heavenly Father. When you give alms, do not blow a trumpet before you, as the hypocrites do in the synagogues and in the streets to win the praise of others. Amen, I say to you, they have received their reward. But when you give alms, do not let your left hand know what your right is doing, so that your almsgiving may be secret. And your Father who sees in secret will repay you.

"When you pray, do not be like the hypocrites, who love to stand and pray in the synagogues and on street corners so that others may see them. Amen, I say to you, they have received their reward. But when you pray, go to your inner room, close the door, and pray to your Father in secret. And your Father who sees in secret will repay you.

"When you fast, do not look gloomy like the hypocrites. They neglect their appearance, so that they may appear to others to be fasting. Amen, I say

> to you, they have received their reward. But when you fast, anoint your head and wash your face, so that you may not appear to be fasting, except to your Father who is hidden. And your Father who sees what is hidden will repay you."

Friends, in today's Gospel, the Lord prescribes prayer, fasting, and almsgiving as our Lenten disciplines.

The Church traditionally says there are three things we ought to do during Lent, and I put stress on the word *do*. In recent years, we've emphasized the interior dimensions a little too much—that Lent is primarily about attitudes, about ideas and intentions. In the traditional practice of the Church, Lent is about doing things, things that involve the body as much as the mind, that involve the exterior of your life as much as the interior.

The three great practices of Lent—prayer, fasting, and almsgiving—are three things you do. This is going to sound a little bit strange, but my recommendation for this Lent is, in a certain way, to forget about your spiritual life—by which I mean forget about looking inside at how you're progressing spiritually. Follow the Church's recommendations and do three things: pray, fast, and give alms. And as you do, pray to draw closer to the Lord as the center of your life—and the reason you do everything.

**Reflect:** How do you think the practices of Lent, specifically prayer, fasting, and almsgiving, can lead us to a deeper relationship with Christ?

_____

_____

_____

_____

_____

_____

_____

_____

_____

_____

_____

_____

_____

_____

_____

# FEBRUARY 15, 2024

**Thursday after Ash Wednesday**

### Luke 9:22–25

J esus said to his disciples: "The Son of Man must suffer greatly and be rejected by the elders, the chief priests, and the scribes, and be killed and on the third day be raised."

Then he said to all, "If anyone wishes to come after me, he must deny himself and take up his cross daily and follow me. For whoever wishes to save his life will lose it, but whoever loses his life for my sake will save it. What profit is there for one to gain the whole world yet lose or forfeit himself?"

Friends, our Gospel today lays out Jesus' conditions for discipleship. For all of us sinners, to varying degrees, our own lives have become god. That is to say, we see the universe turning around our ego, our needs, our projects, our plans, and our likes and dislikes. True conversion—the *metanoia* that Jesus talks about—is so much more than moral reform, though it includes that. It has to do with a complete shift in consciousness, a whole new way of looking at one's life.

Jesus offered a teaching that must have been gut-wrenching to his first-century audience: "If anyone wishes to come after me, he must deny himself and take up his cross daily and follow me." His listeners knew what the cross meant: a death in utter agony, nakedness, and humiliation. They didn't think of the cross automatically in religious terms, as we do. They knew it in all of its awful power.

Unless you crucify your ego, you cannot be my follower, Jesus says. This move—this terrible move—has to be the foundation of the spiritual life.

**Reflect:** Where is your ego overly dominant? What do you have to do to crucify it?

# FEBRUARY 16, 2024

## Friday after Ash Wednesday

### Matthew 9:14–15

The disciples of John approached Jesus and said, "Why do we and the Pharisees fast much, but your disciples do not fast?" Jesus answered them, "Can the wedding guests mourn as long as the bridegroom is with them? The days will come when the bridegroom is taken away from them, and then they will fast."

Friends, in today's Gospel, people ask Jesus why his disciples do not fast. He says that as wedding guests, they will not fast while he, the Bridegroom, is with them. But "the days will come," he says, "when the bridegroom is taken away from them, and then they will fast."

Why do we fast? Because we have a hunger for God, which is the deepest hunger. We're meant to get access to that hunger. We're meant to feel it so that it can direct us toward God. Every spiritual master recognizes the danger that if we allow the superficial hunger of our lives to dominate, we never reach the deepest hunger.

Thomas Merton once observed that our desires for food and drink are something like little children in their persistence and tendency to dominate. Unless and until they are disciplined, they will skew the functions of the soul according to their purposes.

And fasting is a way of disciplining the hunger for food and drink. It is a way of quieting those desires by not responding to them immediately, so that the deepest desires emerge. Unless you fast, you might never realize how hungry you are for God.

**Reflect:** Why do we fast during Lent? How does this practice affect you?

# FEBRUARY 17, 2024

## Saturday after Ash Wednesday

### Luke 5:27–32

Jesus saw a tax collector named Levi sitting at the customs post. He said to him, "Follow me." And leaving everything behind, he got up and followed him. Then Levi gave a great banquet for him in his house, and a large crowd of tax collectors and others were at table with them. The Pharisees and their scribes complained to his disciples, saying, "Why do you eat and drink with tax collectors and sinners?" Jesus said to them in reply, "Those who are healthy do not need a physician, but the sick do. I have not come to call the righteous to repentance but sinners."

Friends, today's Gospel tells the story of the Lord calling Levi, also known as Matthew. As Jesus was passing by, he spotted Matthew at his tax collector's post. To be a tax collector in Jesus' time—a Jew collaborating with Rome's oppression of one's own people—was to be a contemptible figure.

Jesus gazed at Matthew and simply said, "Follow me." Did Jesus invite Matthew because the tax collector merited it? Was Jesus responding to a request from Matthew or some longing in the sinner's heart? Certainly not. Grace, by definition, comes unbidden and without explanation.

In Caravaggio's magnificent painting of this scene, Matthew, dressed anachronistically in sixteenth-century finery, responds to Jesus' summons by pointing incredulously to himself and wearing a quizzical expression, as if to say, "Me? You want me?"

Just as creation is *ex nihilo*, so conversion is a new creation, a gracious remaking of a person from the nonbeing of his sin. Matthew, we are told, immediately got up and followed the Lord.

**Reflect:** Reflect on a time in your life when grace came to you "unbidden and without explanation."

_____

_____

_____

_____

_____

_____

_____

_____

_____

_____

_____

_____

# FEBRUARY 18, 2024

**First Sunday of Lent**

### Mark 1:12–15

The Spirit drove Jesus out into the desert, and he remained in the desert for forty days, tempted by Satan. He was among wild beasts, and the angels ministered to him.

After John had been arrested, Jesus came to Galilee proclaiming the gospel of God: "This is the time of fulfillment. The kingdom of God is at hand. Repent, and believe in the gospel."

Friends, in today's Gospel, Jesus goes into Galilee and begins to preach. The first words out of his mouth, as Mark reports them, serve as a sort of summary statement of his life and work: "This is the time of fulfillment. The kingdom of God is at hand. Repent, and believe in the gospel."

The moment has arrived, the privileged time, the *kairos*; something that human beings have been longing for and striving after and hoping to see has appeared, and the time is now for a decision, for action. Jesus' very first words are a wake-up call, a warning bell in the night, a summons to attention. This is not the time to be asleep, not the time to be languishing in complacency and self-satisfaction, not the time for delaying tactics, for procrastination and second guessing.

In the Byzantine liturgy, we find the oft-repeated call to "be attentive," and in the Buddhist tradition, there is a great emphasis placed on wakefulness. In the fiction of James Joyce, we often find that moments of spiritual insight are preceded by a great thunderclap, the cosmic alarm shocking the characters (and the reader) into wide-awakeness. The initial words of Jesus' first sermon are a similar invitation to psychological and spiritual awareness: there is something to be seen, so open your eyes!

**Reflect:** What are your hopes, dreams, and longings? How does Jesus fulfill them?

_____

_____

_____

_____

_____

_____

_____

_____

_____

_____

# FEBRUARY 19, 2024

Monday of the First Week of Lent

### Matthew 25:31–46

Jesus said to his disciples: "When the Son of Man comes in his glory, and all the angels with him, he will sit upon his glorious throne, and all the nations will be assembled before him. And he will separate them one from another, as a shepherd separates the sheep from the goats. He will place the sheep on his right and the goats on his left. Then the king will say to those on his right, 'Come, you who are blessed by my Father. Inherit the kingdom prepared for you from the foundation of the world. For I was hungry and you gave me food, I was thirsty and you gave me drink, a stranger and you welcomed me, naked and you clothed me, ill and you cared for me, in prison and you visited me.' Then the righteous will answer him and say, 'Lord, when did we see you hungry and feed you, or thirsty and give you drink? When did we see you a stranger and welcome you, or naked and clothe you? When did we see you ill or in prison, and visit you?' And the king will say to them in reply, 'Amen, I say to you, whatever you did for one of these least brothers of mine, you did for me.' Then he will say to those on his left, 'Depart from me, you accursed, into the eternal fire prepared for the Devil and his angels. For I was hungry and you gave me no food, I was thirsty and you gave me no drink, a stranger and you gave me no welcome, naked and you gave me no clothing, ill and in prison, and you did not care for me.' Then they will answer and say, 'Lord, when did we see you hungry or thirsty or a stranger or naked or ill or in prison, and not minister to your needs?' He will answer them, 'Amen, I say to you, what you did not do for one of these least ones, you did not do for me.' And these will go off to eternal punishment, but the righteous to eternal life."

Friends, in our Gospel today, Jesus tells the crowd that the Son of Man will welcome the righteous into the kingdom, saying, "For I was hungry and you gave me food, I was thirsty and you gave me drink, a stranger and you welcomed me, naked and you clothed me, ill and you cared for me, in prison and you visited me." Puzzled, the righteous will ask when they did this, and he will reply, "Whatever you did for one of these least brothers of mine, you did for me."

This is a powerful evocation of Jesus' teaching about the mutuality of our love for God and neighbor. The absolute love for God is not in competition with a radical commitment to love our fellow human beings, precisely because God is not one being among many, but the very ground of our existence.

Someone who operated very much in the spirit of this teaching was St. Teresa of Kolkata. A writer was once conversing with her, searching out the sources of her spirituality and mission. At the end of their long talk, she asked him to spread his hand out on the table. Touching his fingers one by one as she spoke the words, she said, "You did it to me."

**Reflect:** How are good works an integral part of claiming to believe in Jesus Christ?

_____

_____

_____

_____

_____

_____

_____

_____

_____

_____

_____

# FEBRUARY 20, 2024

## Tuesday of the First Week of Lent

### Matthew 6:7–15

Jesus said to his disciples: "In praying, do not babble like the pagans, who think that they will be heard because of their many words. Do not be like them. Your Father knows what you need before you ask him.

"This is how you are to pray:

> Our Father who art in heaven,
>     hallowed be thy name,
>         thy Kingdom come,
> thy will be done,
>     on earth as it is in heaven.
> Give us this day our daily bread;
> and forgive us our trespasses,
>     as we forgive those who trespass against us;
> and lead us not into temptation,
>     but deliver us from evil.

"If you forgive men their transgressions, your heavenly Father will forgive you. But if you do not forgive men, neither will your Father forgive your transgressions."

Friends, today's Gospel is Matthew's version of the Lord's Prayer. I want to reflect on the first verses. How wonderful that, in Luke's version, it comes directly from the prayer of Jesus himself. It is as though the prayer that he teaches them sums up the content of his own prayer.

We call God "Father" when we pray. We call him Abba, Daddy. The same intimacy that Jesus has with his Abba he invites us to share. We don't just imitate his prayer, the way we would imitate the prayer of any spiritual teacher; rather, we enter into the dynamics of his own being when we pray.

"Hallowed be thy name." May your name be held holy. The first thing we ask is that we might honor him, that we might make him first in our lives, that he might be set apart from everything else. Job, family, money, success, the esteem of others, our friends—all of it is good, but none of it is to be held holy in this sense.

If we get this wrong, we get everything else wrong. If we don't hold his name holy above all, everything becomes profane.

**Reflect:** What does it mean to "hold God's name holy above all" in your own life? Is anything competing for that top position of honor?

**Wednesday of the First Week of Lent**

### Luke 11:29–32

While still more people gathered in the crowd, Jesus said to them, "This generation is an evil generation; it seeks a sign, but no sign will be given it, except the sign of Jonah. Just as Jonah became a sign to the Ninevites, so will the Son of Man be to this generation. At the judgment the queen of the south will rise with the men of this generation and she will condemn them, because she came from the ends of the earth to hear the wisdom of Solomon, and there is something greater than Solomon here. At the judgment the men of Nineveh will arise with this generation and condemn it, because at the preaching of Jonah they repented, and there is something greater than Jonah here."

Friends, in today's Gospel, Jesus tells the crowd that the only sign he will give is the sign of Jonah—the victory of his death and Resurrection.

If Jesus had died and simply remained in his grave, he would be remembered (if he was remembered at all) as a noble idealist, tragically crushed by the forces of history. There could have been, in the first century, no surer sign that someone was *not* the

Messiah than his death at the hands of the enemies of Israel, for one of the central marks of messiahship was precisely victory over those enemies.

That Peter, James, John, Paul, and the rest could announce throughout the Mediterranean world that Jesus was in fact the long-awaited Israelite Messiah, and that they could go to their deaths defending this claim, are the surest indications that something monumentally significant happened to Jesus after his death.

That something was the Resurrection. Though too many modern theologians have tried to explain the Resurrection away as a wish-fulfilling fantasy, a vague symbol, or a literary invention, the New Testament writers could not be clearer: the crucified Jesus, who had died and been buried, appeared alive again to his disciples.

**Reflect:** Where would your faith be without belief in the Resurrection?

# FEBRUARY 22, 2024

*Feast of the Chair of Saint Peter, Apostle*

### Matthew 16:13–19

When Jesus went into the region of Caesarea Philippi he asked his disciples, "Who do people say that the Son of Man is?" They replied, "Some say John the Baptist, others Elijah, still others Jeremiah or one of the prophets." He said to them, "But who do you say that I am?" Simon Peter said in reply, "You are the Christ, the Son of the living God." Jesus said to him in reply, "Blessed are you, Simon son of Jonah. For flesh and blood has not revealed this to you, but my heavenly Father. And so I say to you, you are Peter, and upon this rock I will build my Church, and the gates of the netherworld shall not prevail against it. I will give you the keys to the Kingdom of heaven. Whatever you bind on earth shall be bound in heaven; and whatever you loose on earth shall be loosed in heaven."

Friends, today's Gospel spells out the importance of Peter's confession. For it is upon this inspired confession that the Church is built. Not, mind you, on popular opinion, which is shifting and indecisive, and not on personal holiness, which is all too rare. It is built upon the inspired authority of Peter—and I say, "Thank God!"

We make this troubling and extraordinary claim that it is through a special charism of the Spirit that Peter and his successors govern the Church. Now, I realize that I have many Protestant readers and that this text has been, between Catholics and Protestants, a stumbling block. Let me clarify what is and is not at stake here.

What is the focus of Peter's confession? It has to do with who Jesus is. This is the rock upon which the Church is built. We don't say for a moment that all of Peter's practical decisions are right, that everything he says is right. But we are saying that he is right about who Jesus is: a man who is also the Son of the living God. And this is the source and ground of the whole operation.

**Reflect:** Reflect on this and other Gospel stories about Peter. In what ways is he an appropriate archetype of the Church?

_____

_____

_____

_____

_____

_____

_____

# FEBRUARY 23, 2024

### Friday of the First Week of Lent

### Matthew 5:20–26

Jesus said to his disciples: "I tell you, unless your righteousness surpasses that of the scribes and Pharisees, you will not enter into the Kingdom of heaven.

"You have heard that it was said to your ancestors, *You shall not kill; and whoever kills will be liable to judgment.* But I say to you, whoever is angry with his brother will be liable to judgment, and whoever says to his brother, *Raqa*, will be answerable to the Sanhedrin, and whoever says, 'You fool,' will be liable to fiery Gehenna. Therefore, if you bring your gift to the altar, and there recall that your brother has anything against you, leave your gift there at the altar, go first and be reconciled with your brother, and then come and offer your gift. Settle with your opponent quickly while on the way to court. Otherwise your opponent will hand you over to the judge, and the judge will hand you over to the guard, and you will be thrown into prison. Amen, I say to you, you will not be released until you have paid the last penny."

Friends, in today's Gospel, Jesus commands us to be reconciled with one another. I want to say something about the role of forgiveness in repairing our broken relationships.

When you are at worship and realize that you need to forgive someone (or be forgiven by someone), go and do it. Go get reconciled, then come back. It's like a rule of physics. There is something hidden in the deep mystery of God, and I can't fully explicate it. Somehow, if there is a lack of forgiveness in you, it blocks the movement of God in you. Perhaps it's simply because God is love, and so whatever is opposed to love in us blocks the flow of God's power and God's life.

One reason we do not forgive is that we feel that some injustice has been done to us, and we resent it. A good cure for this feeling is to kneel before the cross of Jesus. What do you see there? The innocent Son of God nailed to the cross—the ultimate injustice. What does he do? He forgives his persecutors. Meditate on that, and your sense of being treated unjustly will fade away.

**Reflect:** Is there a lack of forgiveness in you somewhere? Follow Bishop Barron's suggestion to kneel before the cross of Jesus often during Lent and see what happens.

# FEBRUARY 24, 2024

**Saturday of the First Week of Lent**

### Matthew 5:43–48

Jesus said to his disciples: "You have heard that it was said, *You shall love your neighbor and hate your enemy.* But I say to you, love your enemies, and pray for those who persecute you, that you may be children of your heavenly Father, for he makes his sun rise on the bad and the good, and causes rain to fall on the just and the unjust. For if you love those who love you, what recompense will you have? Do not the tax collectors do the same? And if you greet your brothers and sisters only, what is unusual about that? Do not the pagans do the same? So be perfect, just as your heavenly Father is perfect."

Friends, today's Gospel tells us to love our enemies so that we may be like the Father. What is the Father of Jesus Christ like? Well, listen: "He makes his sun rise on the bad and the good, and causes rain to fall on the just and the unjust." The Father of Jesus Christ *is* love, right through. That's all God is; that's all he knows how to do. He is not like us: unstable, changing, moving from one attitude to another. No, God simply *is* love.

In every case, his grace comes first, and grace is all that he has to give. This is why the comparison to the sun and the rain is so apt. The sun doesn't ask who deserves its warmth or its light before it shines. It just shines, and both good and bad people receive it. Neither does the rain inquire as to the moral rectitude of those upon whom it showers its life-giving goodness. It just pours—and both just and unjust people receive it.

**Reflect:** Have you ever asked God to give you the grace to love "unlovable" people the way he loves them? If so, what happened? If you have not asked him for this grace, why not?

# FEBRUARY 25, 2024

## Second Sunday of Lent

### Mark 9:2–10

Jesus took Peter, James, and John and led them up a high mountain apart by themselves. And he was transfigured before them, and his clothes became dazzling white, such as no fuller on earth could bleach them. Then Elijah appeared to them along with Moses, and they were conversing with Jesus. Then Peter said to Jesus in reply, "Rabbi, it is good that we are here! Let us make three tents: one for you, one for Moses, and one for Elijah." He hardly knew what to say, they were so terrified. Then a cloud came, casting a shadow over them; from the cloud came a voice, "This is my beloved Son. Listen to him." Suddenly, looking around, they no longer saw anyone but Jesus alone with them.

As they were coming down from the mountain, he charged them not to relate what they had seen to anyone, except when the Son of Man had risen from the dead. So they kept the matter to themselves, questioning what rising from the dead meant.

Friends, today's Gospel presents the Transfiguration of Christ. What is the Transfiguration itself? Mark speaks literally of a metamorphosis, a going beyond the form that he had. If I can use Paul's language, it is "the knowledge of the glory of God on the face of Jesus Christ." In and through his humble humanity, his divinity shines forth. The proximity of his divinity in no way compromises the integrity of his humanity, but rather makes it shine in greater beauty. This is the New Testament version of the burning bush.

The Jesus who is both divine and human is the Jesus who is evangelically compelling. If he is only divine, then he doesn't touch us; if he is only human, he can't save us. His splendor consists in the coming together of the two natures, without mixing, mingling, or confusion.

This same Jesus then accompanies his disciples back down the mountain and walks with them in the ordinary rhythms of their lives. This is the Christ who wants to reign as Lord of our lives in every detail. If we forget about this dimension, then Jesus becomes a distant memory, a figure from the past.

**Reflect:** How does the truth that humanity and divinity meet in Jesus affect your understanding of humanity? Of divinity?

# *FEBRUARY 26, 2024*

**Monday of the Second Week of Lent**

Luke 6:36–38

Jesus said to his disciples: "Be merciful, just as your Father is merciful.

"Stop judging and you will not be judged. Stop condemning and you will not be condemned. Forgive and you will be forgiven. Give and gifts will be given to you; a good measure, packed together, shaken down, and overflowing, will be poured into your lap. For the measure with which you measure will in return be measured out to you."

Friends, in today's Gospel, Jesus charges us to be merciful and to stop judging others. But we cannot perform such behaviors on our own strength—we need God's assistance.

In the Sermon on the Mount in Matthew, Jesus tells his followers: "Be perfect, therefore, as your heavenly Father is perfect." The perfection that he urges—which includes a radical love of enemies, the practice of nonviolence in the face of aggression, the refusal to judge one's brothers and sisters, and an embrace of poverty, meekness, and simplicity of heart—is not desirable or even possible within a natural framework.

The form of life outlined in the Sermon on the Mount would strike Aristotle as excessive and irrational—and that is just the point. Its viability and beauty will emerge only when one's mind, will, and body have been invaded and elevated by the love that God is.

This is not to say that the natural moral excellences perceived by Aristotle are invalidated by grace; the invasion of the sacred does not overwhelm or undermine the secular. But it does indeed transfigure it. This transfiguration is the effect of love, working its way through the moral self.

**Reflect:** When faced with the command of Jesus to "be perfect," do you try harder, give up, or surrender to grace? If you surrender, what does that surrender look like?

_____

_____

_____

_____

_____

_____

_____

_____

_____

# FEBRUARY 27, 2024

**Tuesday of the Second Week of Lent**

### Matthew 23:1–12

Jesus spoke to the crowds and to his disciples, saying, "The scribes and the Pharisees have taken their seat on the chair of Moses. Therefore, do and observe all things whatsoever they tell you, but do not follow their example. For they preach but they do not practice. They tie up heavy burdens hard to carry and lay them on people's shoulders, but they will not lift a finger to move them. All their works are performed to be seen. They widen their phylacteries and lengthen their tassels. They love places of honor at banquets, seats of honor in synagogues, greetings in marketplaces, and the salutation 'Rabbi.' As for you, do not be called 'Rabbi.' You have but one teacher, and you are all brothers. Call no one on earth your father; you have but one Father in heaven. Do not be called 'Master'; you have but one master, the Christ. The greatest among you must be your servant. Whoever exalts himself will be humbled; but whoever humbles himself will be exalted."

Friends, today's Gospel exposes the pride of the Pharisees and concludes with the prescription of humility. I want to reflect on this virtue.

St. Augustine said that all of us, made from nothing, tend toward nothing. We can see this in our frailty and sin and mortality. St. Paul said, "What do you possess that you have not received? But if you have received it, why are you boasting as if you did not receive it?"

To believe in God is to know these truths. To live them out is to live in the attitude of humility. Thomas Aquinas said *humilitas veritas*, meaning humility is truth. It is living out the deepest truth of things: God is God, and we are not.

Now, all of this sounds very clear when it's stated in this abstract manner, but man is it hard to live out! In our fallen world, we forget so readily that we are creatures. We start to assume that we are gods, the center of the universe.

The ego becomes a massive monkey on our backs, and it has to be fed and pampered constantly. What a liberation it is to let go of the ego! Do you see why humility is not a degradation, but an elevation?

**Reflect:** What do you possess that you have not received?

---

---

---

### Matthew 20:17–28

As Jesus was going up to Jerusalem, he took the Twelve disciples aside by themselves, and said to them on the way, "Behold, we are going up to Jerusalem, and the Son of Man will be handed over to the chief priests and the scribes, and they will condemn him to death, and hand him over to the Gentiles to be mocked and scourged and crucified, and he will be raised on the third day."

Then the mother of the sons of Zebedee approached Jesus with her sons and did him homage, wishing to ask him for something. He said to her, "What do you wish?" She answered him, "Command that these two sons of mine sit, one at your right and the other at your left, in your kingdom." Jesus said in reply, "You do not know what you are asking. Can you drink the chalice that I am going to drink?" They said to him, "We can." He replied, "My chalice you will indeed drink, but to sit at my right and at my left, this is not mine to give but is for those for whom it has been prepared by my Father." When the ten heard this, they became indignant at the two brothers. But Jesus

> summoned them and said, "You know that the rulers of the Gentiles lord it over them, and the great ones make their authority over them felt. But it shall not be so among you. Rather, whoever wishes to be great among you shall be your servant; whoever wishes to be first among you shall be your slave. Just so, the Son of Man did not come to be served but to serve and to give his life as a ransom for many."

Friends, in today's Gospel, the mother of James and John asks Jesus in their name that they be honored in his kingdom.

Jesus patiently attends to their request and tries to clarify and redirect it. Then his final answer comes: "But to sit at my right and at my left, this is not mine to give but is for those for whom it has been prepared by my Father."

The Father has prepared the place for one who will reign with Jesus when he comes into his glory. On Good Friday afternoon, the good thief turned to the crucified Jesus and made a request that was similar to that of James and John: "Jesus, remember me when you come into your kingdom." And to him Jesus responded, "Amen, I say to you, today you will be with me in Paradise."

This crucified criminal was indeed in the very place that James and John, in their naïve ambition, coveted. The one who was drinking the same cup of suffering as Jesus was privileged to reign with him. Let there be no limit to your ambition, as long as it conduces you to that place alongside the crucified Christ.

**Reflect:** Are you drinking your cup of suffering alongside Jesus? If so, how do you think and feel about that suffering?

_____

_____

_____

_____

_____

_____

_____

_____

_____

_____

_____

_____

_____

_____

_____

_____

# FEBRUARY 29, 2024

## Thursday of the Second Week of Lent

### Luke 16:19–31

Jesus said to the Pharisees: "There was a rich man who dressed in purple garments and fine linen and dined sumptuously each day. And lying at his door was a poor man named Lazarus, covered with sores, who would gladly have eaten his fill of the scraps that fell from the rich man's table. Dogs even used to come and lick his sores. When the poor man died, he was carried away by angels to the bosom of Abraham. The rich man also died and was buried, and from the netherworld, where he was in torment, he raised his eyes and saw Abraham far off and Lazarus at his side. And he cried out, 'Father Abraham, have pity on me. Send Lazarus to dip the tip of his finger in water and cool my tongue, for I am suffering torment in these flames.' Abraham replied, 'My child, remember that you received what was good during your lifetime while Lazarus likewise received what was bad; but now he is comforted here, whereas you are tormented. Moreover, between us and you a great chasm is established to prevent anyone from crossing who might wish to go from our side to yours or from your side to ours.' He said, 'Then I beg you, father, send him to my father's house, for I have five brothers, so that he may warn

> them, lest they too come to this place of torment.' But Abraham replied, 'They have Moses and the prophets. Let them listen to them.' He said, 'Oh no, father Abraham, but if someone from the dead goes to them, they will repent.' Then Abraham said, 'If they will not listen to Moses and the prophets, neither will they be persuaded if someone should rise from the dead.'"

Friends, today's Gospel reading is the story of the poor man Lazarus, who sat outside the door of a rich man and "would gladly have eaten his fill of the scraps that fell from the rich man's table." The rich man isn't named, and that's very interesting. In the ancient world, the rich and powerful were the ones who deserved to have their names mentioned. Whose names weren't mentioned? The poor and the marginalized. So this is a very interesting reversal that is going on here.

And we know this story well, right? Day after day, the rich man walks past Lazarus, in and out of his house. When Lazarus dies, he's taken to the "bosom of Abraham." But the rich man dies and he's taken to the underworld. Again another reversal. You'd expect that God has blessed the rich and powerful and cursed those who are poor and hopeless. But that's not the way the Bible imagines this situation. It's Lazarus who's carried to paradise and the rich man who's carried downward.

There's the revolutionary quality of the Bible, turning our expectations upside down. How much do we care for those who are poor? Can we name them, or are they for us, as for ancient peoples, just a nameless mass of suffering people? And are we committed to helping these people by performing the corporal works of mercy?

**Reflect:** Make a list of how you use your material possessions for the common good. Try to add to that list before Easter.

_____

_____

_____

_____

_____

_____

_____

_____

_____

_____

_____

_____

### Matthew 21:33–43, 45–46

Jesus said to the chief priests and the elders of the people: "Hear another parable. There was a landowner who planted a vineyard, put a hedge around it, dug a wine press in it, and built a tower. Then he leased it to tenants and went on a journey. When vintage time drew near, he sent his servants to the tenants to obtain his produce. But the tenants seized the servants and one they beat, another they killed, and a third they stoned. Again he sent other servants, more numerous than the first ones, but they treated them in the same way. Finally, he sent his son to them, thinking, 'They will respect my son.' But when the tenants saw the son, they said to one another, 'This is the heir. Come, let us kill him and acquire his inheritance.' They seized him, threw him out of the vineyard, and killed him. What will the owner of the vineyard do to those tenants when he comes?" They answered him, "He will put those wretched men to a wretched death and lease his vineyard to other tenants who will give him the produce at the proper times." Jesus said to them,

"Did you never read in the Scriptures:
*The stone that the builders rejected*
*has become the cornerstone;*
*by the Lord has this been done,*
*and it is wonderful in our eyes?*
Therefore, I say to you, the Kingdom of God will be taken away from you and given to a people that will produce its fruit." When the chief priests and the Pharisees heard his parables, they knew that he was speaking about them. And although they were attempting to arrest him, they feared the crowds, for they regarded him as a prophet.

Friends, in today's Gospel, Jesus tells the parable of the tenants. This is one of the most terrible anticipations of the cross. In a final attempt to make his vineyard fruitful, God sent his only begotten Son, but even he was rejected.

How are *we* tending the vineyard? We have received so much from God, but are we making the world fruitful? Are we responding to the Lord's invitation with the works of justice, love, peace, chastity, respect for others? Or are we more or less killing the messengers?

There are many ways to look at contemporary secularism and relativism. A secularist world is one that has grown intentionally deaf to the voice of the Spirit. St. John Paul II called it "the culture of death." God, as is his wont, allows us to feel the effects of our sin.

Okay, but we are never meant to read the Gospel and end up depressed. The Gospel is always Good News. God has not given up on us! He turns the sign of defeat into the sign of victory. The very one whom we reject is the one whom he gives back to us as a source of life.

**Reflect:** Have you ever turned your back on God? How did he pursue you and bring you back to himself?

_____

_____

_____

_____

_____

_____

_____

_____

_____

_____

# MARCH 2, 2024

**Saturday of the Second Week of Lent**

### Luke 15:1–3, 11–32

Tax collectors and sinners were all drawing near to listen to Jesus, but the Pharisees and scribes began to complain, saying, "This man welcomes sinners and eats with them." So to them Jesus addressed this parable. "A man had two sons, and the younger son said to his father, 'Father, give me the share of your estate that should come to me.' So the father divided the property between them. After a few days, the younger son collected all his belongings and set off to a distant country where he squandered his inheritance on a life of dissipation. When he had freely spent everything, a severe famine struck that country, and he found himself in dire need. So he hired himself out to one of the local citizens who sent him to his farm to tend the swine. And he longed to eat his fill of the pods on which the swine fed, but nobody gave him any. Coming to his senses he thought, 'How many of my father's hired workers have more than enough food to eat, but here am I, dying from hunger. I shall get up and go to my father and I shall say to him, "Father, I have sinned against heaven and against you. I no longer deserve to be called your son; treat me as you would treat one of your hired workers.'" So he got up and went back to his father. While he was still a long way off, his father caught sight of him, and was filled with compassion. He ran to his son, embraced him and kissed him. His son said to him, 'Father, I have sinned against heaven and against you; I no longer deserve to be called your son.' But his father ordered his servants, 'Quickly, bring the finest robe and put it on him; put a ring on his finger and sandals on his feet. Take the fattened calf and slaughter it. Then let us celebrate with a feast, because this son of mine was dead, and has come to life again; he was lost, and has been found.' Then the celebration began. Now the older son had been out in the field and, on his way back, as he neared the house, he heard the sound of music and dancing. He called one of the servants and asked what this might mean. The servant said to him, 'Your brother has returned and your father has slaughtered the fattened calf because he has him back safe and sound.' He became angry, and when he refused to enter the house, his father came out and pleaded with him. He said to his father in reply, 'Look, all these years I served you and not once did I disobey your orders; yet you never gave me even a young goat to feast on with my friends. But when your son returns who swallowed up your property with prostitutes, for him you slaughter the fattened calf.' He said to him, 'My son, you are here with me always; everything I have is yours. But now we must celebrate and rejoice, because your brother was dead and has come to life again; he was lost and has been found.'"

Friends, at the core of today's Gospel is a portrait of our God, who is prodigal. The father stands for the God whose very nature is to give, the God who simply *is* love. And the younger son stands for all of us sinners who tend to misunderstand how to access the divine love.

Since God exists only in gift form, his life, even in principle, cannot become a possession. Instead, it is "had" only on the fly, only in the measure that it is given away. When we cling to it, it disappears, according to a kind of spiritual physics.

The Greek that lies behind "distant country" in the parable is *chora makra*; that means, literally, "the great emptiness." Trying to turn the divine gift into the ego's possession necessarily results in nothing, nonbeing, the void.

St. John Paul II formulated the principle here as "the law of the gift"—that your being increases inasmuch as you give it away. If clinging and possessing are the marks of the *chora makra*, then the law of the gift is the defining dynamic of the father's house, where the robe and the ring and the fatted calf are on permanent offer.

**Reflect:** What gifts do you have that you give away freely? What gifts do you cling to?

_____

_____

_____

_____

_____

_____

_____

_____

_____

_____

_____

_____

_____

_____

_____

# MARCH 3, 2024

**Third Sunday of Lent**

### John 2:13–25

Since the Passover of the Jews was near, Jesus went up to Jerusalem. He found in the temple area those who sold oxen, sheep, and doves, as well as the money changers seated there. He made a whip out of cords and drove them all out of the temple area, with the sheep and oxen, and spilled the coins of the money changers and overturned their tables, and to those who sold doves he said, "Take these out of here, and stop making my Father's house a marketplace." His disciples recalled the words of Scripture, *Zeal for your house will consume me*. At this the Jews answered and said to him, "What sign can you show us for doing this?" Jesus answered and said to them, "Destroy this temple and in three days I will raise it up." The Jews said, "This temple has been under construction for forty-six years, and you will raise it up in three days?" But he was speaking about the temple of his body. Therefore, when he was raised from the dead, his disciples remembered that he had said this, and they came to believe the Scripture and the word Jesus had spoken.

> While he was in Jerusalem for the feast of Passover, many began to believe in his name when they saw the signs he was doing. But Jesus would not trust himself to them because he knew them all, and did not need anyone to testify about human nature. He himself understood it well.

Friends, in today's Gospel, the Jews ask Jesus for a sign, and he blithely comments, "Destroy this temple and in three days I will raise it up." One of the most startling claims that Jesus made about himself is that the people of Israel should come to him for those goods that they formerly sought in the temple: forgiveness, teaching, and healing. And he confirmed this identification when making this statement after purifying the temple of the money changers.

The bystanders remark on the absurdity of this claim, reminding him that the construction of this Herodian version of the sacred place had taken forty-six years. The author of the Gospel provides the indispensable gloss: "But he was speaking about the temple of his body." In a word, Jesus himself is the very particular "place" where the God of Israel, who cannot be contained by the entire universe, deigned in a unique and unrepeatable way to dwell.

The temple known to Jesus and his followers would be obliterated just forty years after the time of Christ. But the temple of Jesus' Body, the Church, will endure forever.

**Reflect:** In what ways does the Church continue Jesus' life-giving ministry?

_____

_____

_____

_____

_____

_____

_____

_____

_____

_____

_____

_____

_____

### Luke 4:24–30

Jesus said to the people in the synagogue at Nazareth: "Amen, I say to you, no prophet is accepted in his own native place. Indeed, I tell you, there were many widows in Israel in the days of Elijah when the sky was closed for three and a half years and a severe famine spread over the entire land. It was to none of these that Elijah was sent, but only to a widow in Zarephath in the land of Sidon. Again, there were many lepers in Israel during the time of Elisha the prophet; yet not one of them was cleansed, but only Naaman the Syrian." When the people in the synagogue heard this, they were all filled with fury. They rose up, drove him out of the town, and led him to the brow of the hill on which their town had been built, to hurl him down headlong. But he passed through the midst of them and went away.

Friends, in today's Gospel, Jesus' hometown rejects him as a prophet. And I want to say a word about your role as a prophet.

When most laypeople hear about prophecy, they sit back and their eyes glaze over. "That's something for the priests and the bishops to worry about; they're the modern-day prophets. I don't have that call or that responsibility."

Well, think again! Vatican II emphasized the universal call to holiness, rooted in the dynamics of Baptism. Every baptized person is conformed unto Christ—priest, prophet, and king. Whenever you assist at Mass, you are exercising your priestly office, participating in the worship of God. Whenever you direct your kids to discover their mission in the Church or provide guidance to someone in the spiritual life, you are exercising your kingly office.

As a baptized individual, you are also commissioned as a prophet—which is to say, a speaker of God's truth. And the prophetic word is not your own. It is not the result of your own meditations on the spiritual life, as valuable and correct as those may be. The prophetic word is the word of God given to you by God.

**Reflect:** How would you evaluate your role as prophet—that is, a speaker of God's truth?

_____

_____

_____

_____

_____

# MARCH 5, 2024

Tuesday of the Third Week of Lent

### Matthew 18:21–35

Peter approached Jesus and asked him, "Lord, if my brother sins against me, how often must I forgive him? As many as seven times?" Jesus answered, "I say to you, not seven times but seventy-seven times. That is why the Kingdom of heaven may be likened to a king who decided to settle accounts with his servants. When he began the accounting, a debtor was brought before him who owed him a huge amount. Since he had no way of paying it back, his master ordered him to be sold, along with his wife, his children, and all his property, in payment of the debt. At that, the servant fell down, did him homage, and said, 'Be patient with me, and I will pay you back in full.' Moved with compassion the master of that servant let him go and forgave him the loan. When that servant had left, he found one of his fellow servants who owed him a much smaller amount. He seized him and started to choke him, demanding, 'Pay back what you owe.' Falling to his knees, his fellow servant begged him, 'Be patient with me, and I will pay you back.' But he refused.

Instead, he had him put in prison until he paid back the debt. Now when his fellow servants saw what had happened, they were deeply disturbed, and went to their master and reported the whole affair. His master summoned him and said to him, 'You wicked servant! I forgave you your entire debt because you begged me to. Should you not have had pity on your fellow servant, as I had pity on you?' Then in anger his master handed him over to the torturers until he should pay back the whole debt. So will my heavenly Father do to you, unless each of you forgives your brother from your heart."

Friends, in today's Gospel, Jesus tells a parable that illustrates God's mercy. The Latin word for mercy is *misericordia*, which designates the suffering of the heart, or compassion—*cum patior* (I suffer with).

Mercy is identical to what the Old Testament authors refer to as God's *hesed*, or tender mercy. It is *the* characteristic of God, for God is love. The love that obtains among the Trinitarian persons spills over into God's love for the world that he has made.

Think of a mother's love for her children. Could you ever imagine a mother becoming indifferent to one of her offspring? But even should she forget, we read in the prophet Isaiah, God will never forget his own. Consider the fact that nothing would exist were it not willed into being by God. But God has no need of anything; hence, his sustaining of the universe is an act of disinterested love and tender mercy.

There is no greater manifestation of the divine mercy than the forgiveness of sins. When G.K. Chesterton was asked why he became a Catholic, he answered, "To have my sins forgiven." This is the greatest grace the Church can offer: reconciliation, the restoration of the divine friendship, the forgiveness of our sins.

**Reflect:** How can you extend God's mercy to someone in your life?

_____

_____

_____

_____

_____

_____

_____

# MARCH 6, 2024

### Wednesday of the Third Week of Lent

**Matthew 5:17–19**

Jesus said to his disciples: "Do not think that I have come to abolish the law or the prophets. I have come not to abolish but to fulfill. Amen, I say to you, until heaven and earth pass away, not the smallest letter or the smallest part of a letter will pass from the law, until all things have taken place. Therefore, whoever breaks one of the least of these commandments and teaches others to do so will be called least in the Kingdom of heaven. But whoever obeys and teaches these commandments will be called greatest in the Kingdom of heaven."

Friends, in today's Gospel, Jesus declares that he has come to fulfill the Law.

The same Jesus who railed against the hypocritical legalism of the Pharisees also said, "I have come not to abolish the law but to fulfill it." And the same Jesus who threatened to tear down the temple in Jerusalem also promised to "raise it up" in three days.

The point is this: Jesus certainly criticized the corruption in the institutional religion of his time, but he by no means called for its wholesale dismantling. He was a loyal, observant, law-abiding Jew.

What he effected was a transfiguration of the best of that classical Israelite religion—temple, law, priesthood, sacrifice, covenant—into the institutions, sacraments, practices, and structures of his Mystical Body, the Church.

Lots of New Age devotees today want spirituality without religion, and lots of evangelicals want Jesus without religion. Both end up with abstractions. But the one thing Jesus is not is an abstraction. Rather, he is a spiritual power who makes himself available precisely in the dense institutional particularity of his Mystical Body across space and time. Jesus didn't come to abolish religion; he came to fulfill it.

**Reflect:** What is the difference between criticizing corruption in the Church and calling for its dismantling? How can you follow Jesus' lead and work to address the issues within the Church today?

_____

_____

_____

_____

_____

# MARCH 7, 2024

Thursday of the Third Week of Lent

Luke 11:14–23

Jesus was driving out a demon that was mute, and when the demon had gone out, the mute man spoke and the crowds were amazed. Some of them said, "By the power of Beelzebul, the prince of demons, he drives out demons." Others, to test him, asked him for a sign from heaven. But he knew their thoughts and said to them, "Every kingdom divided against itself will be laid waste and house will fall against house. And if Satan is divided against himself, how will his kingdom stand? For you say that it is by Beelzebul that I drive out demons. If I, then, drive out demons by Beelzebul, by whom do your own people drive them out? Therefore they will be your judges. But if it is by the finger of God that I drive out demons, then the Kingdom of God has come upon you. When a strong man fully armed guards his palace, his possessions are safe. But when one stronger than he attacks and overcomes him, he takes away the armor on which he relied and distributes the spoils. Whoever is not with me is against me, and whoever does not gather with me scatters."

Friends, in today's Gospel, we learn of a person possessed by a demon. Jesus meets the man and drives out the demon, but then is immediately accused of being in league with Satan. Some of the witnesses said, "By the power of Beelzebul, the prince of demons, he drives out demons."

Jesus' response is wonderful in its logic and laconicism: "Every kingdom divided against itself will be laid waste and house will fall against house. And if Satan is divided against himself, how will his kingdom stand?"

The demonic power is always one of scattering. It breaks up communion. But Jesus, as always, is the voice of *communio*, of one bringing things back together.

Think back to Jesus' feeding of the five thousand. Facing a large, hungry crowd, his disciples beg him to "dismiss the crowds so that they can go to the villages and buy food for themselves." But Jesus answers, "There is no need for them to go away; give them some food yourselves."

Whatever drives the Church apart is an echo of this "dismiss the crowds" impulse and a reminder of the demonic tendency to divide. In times of trial and threat, this is a very common instinct. We blame, attack, break up, and disperse. But Jesus is right: "There is no need for them to go away."

**Reflect:** How can you work for unity among all parts of the Body of Christ?

# *MARCH 8, 2024*

### Mark 12:28–34

One of the scribes came to Jesus and asked him,
"Which is the first of all the commandments?" Jesus
replied, "The first is this:

*Hear, O Israel!*
*The Lord our God is Lord alone!*
*You shall love the Lord your God with all your heart,*
*with all your soul,*
*with all your mind,*
*and with all your strength.*

The second is this:

*You shall love your neighbor as yourself.*

There is no other commandment greater than these."
The scribe said to him, "Well said, teacher. You are
right in saying,

*He is One and there is no other than he.*

And *to love him with all your heart,*
*with all your understanding,*
*with all your strength,*
*and to love your neighbor as yourself*

is worth more than all burnt offerings and sacrifices."
And when Jesus saw that he answered with
understanding, he said to him, "You are not far from
the Kingdom of God." And no one dared to ask him
any more questions.

Friends, our Gospel features what the ancient Israelites referred to as the *shema*: "Hear, O Israel, the Lord your God is Lord alone." Could I invite everyone to make an examination of conscience on the basis of the *shema*? Is God the one Lord of your life? Who or what are his rivals for your attention, for your ultimate concern? Or, to turn the question around: Does absolutely everything in your life belong to God?

But people might ask: How do we give ourselves to a reality that we cannot see? This is where the second command of Jesus comes into play. When asked which is the first of all the commandments, Jesus responded with the *shema*, but then he added a second command—namely, "You shall love your neighbor as yourself."

There is a strict logic at work here. When you really love someone, you tend to love, as well, what they love. Well, what does God love? He loves everything and everyone that he has made. So, if you want to love God, and you find this move difficult because God seems so distant, love everyone you come across for the sake of God.

**Reflect:** Is it possible to love God and not love your neighbor? Why not?

### Luke 18:9–14

Jesus addressed this parable to those who were convinced of their own righteousness and despised everyone else. "Two people went up to the temple area to pray; one was a Pharisee and the other was a tax collector. The Pharisee took up his position and spoke this prayer to himself, 'O God, I thank you that I am not like the rest of humanity—greedy, dishonest, adulterous—or even like this tax collector. I fast twice a week, and I pay tithes on my whole income.' But the tax collector stood off at a distance and would not even raise his eyes to heaven but beat his breast and prayed, 'O God, be merciful to me a sinner.' I tell you, the latter went home justified, not the former; for everyone who exalts himself will be humbled, and the one who humbles himself will be exalted."

Friends, today's Gospel compares the self-centered prayer of the Pharisee with the God-centered prayer of the tax collector.

The Pharisee spoke his prayer to himself. This is, Jesus suggests, a fraudulent, wholly inadequate prayer, precisely because it simply confirms the man in his self-regard. And the god to which he prays is, necessarily, a false god, an idol, since it allows itself to be positioned by the ego-driven needs of the Pharisee.

But then Jesus invites us to meditate upon the tax collector's prayer. He speaks with a simple eloquence: "He beat his breast and prayed, 'O God, be merciful to me a sinner.'" Though it is articulate speech, it is not language that confirms the independence and power of the speaker; just the contrary. It is more of a cry or a groan, an acknowledgment that he needs to receive something, this mysterious mercy for which he begs.

In the first prayer, "god" is the principal member of the audience arrayed before the ego of the Pharisee. But in this second prayer, God is the principal actor, and the tax collector is the audience awaiting a performance the contours of which he cannot fully foresee.

**Reflect:** How does the tenor of your prayers reflect who God is in your life: principal actor or a member of the audience?

_____

_____

_____

_____

_____

_____

# MARCH 10, 2024

**Fourth Sunday of Lent**

### John 3:14–21

J esus said to Nicodemus: "Just as Moses lifted up the serpent in the desert, so must the Son of Man be lifted up, so that everyone who believes in him may have eternal life."

For God so loved the world that he gave his only Son, so that everyone who believes in him might not perish but might have eternal life. For God did not send his Son into the world to condemn the world, but that the world might be saved through him. Whoever believes in him will not be condemned, but whoever does not believe has already been condemned, because he has not believed in the name of the only Son of God. And this is the verdict, that the light came into the world, but people preferred darkness to light, because their works were evil. For everyone who does wicked things hates the light and does not come toward the light, so that his works might not be exposed. But whoever lives the truth comes to the light, so that his works may be clearly seen as done in God.

Friends, our Gospel passage today includes one of Scripture's best-known and best-loved lines. The Lord is speaking to Nicodemus, and we read, "God so loved the world that he gave his only Son, so that everyone who believes in him might not perish but might have eternal life."

Why does the Son come? Because God is angry? Because God wants to lord it over us? Because God needs something? No, he comes purely out of love, out of his desire that we flourish. "For God did not send his Son into the world to condemn the world, but that the world might be saved through him."

It is not in order to work out his anger issues that the Father sends the Son, but that the justice of the world might be restored. Jesus is the fulfillment of God's salvific intent, displayed throughout the Old Testament.

**Reflect:** In what ways have you experienced God's extravagant love?

# MARCH 11, 2024

## Monday of the Fourth Week of Lent

### John 4:43–54

At that time Jesus left [Samaria] for Galilee. For Jesus himself testified that a prophet has no honor in his native place. When he came into Galilee, the Galileans welcomed him, since they had seen all he had done in Jerusalem at the feast; for they themselves had gone to the feast.

Then he returned to Cana in Galilee, where he had made the water wine. Now there was a royal official whose son was ill in Capernaum. When he heard that Jesus had arrived in Galilee from Judea, he went to him and asked him to come down and heal his son, who was near death. Jesus said to him, "Unless you people see signs and wonders, you will not believe." The royal official said to him, "Sir, come down before my child dies." Jesus said to him, "You may go; your son will live." The man believed what Jesus said to him and left. While the man was on his way back, his slaves met him and told him that his boy would live. He asked them when he began to recover. They told him, "The fever left him yesterday, about one in the afternoon." The father realized that just at that time Jesus had said to him, "Your son will live," and he and his whole household came to believe. Now this was the second sign Jesus did when he came to Galilee from Judea.

Friends, in today's Gospel, Jesus heals the son of a royal official.

Healer: that's why he's come; that's who he is. In Jesus, divinity and humanity meet. His whole body—his hands, his mouth, his eyes—becomes a conduit of God's energy. What's God's energy, God's purpose? To set right a world gone wrong, a suffering world. Out of every pore of his body, Jesus expresses the healing love of God.

Jesus' ministry of healing expresses in history God's ultimate intention for the world. In Jesus we see a hint of that world to come where there will be no more suffering, no more sadness, no more sickness.

He does not wait for the sinner, the sufferer, the marginalized to come to him. In love and humility, he goes to them. This same Jesus, risen from the dead, present and alive in the Church, is still seeking us out, coming into our homes—not waiting for us to crawl to him, but seeking us out in love and humility.

**Reflect:** How do you need Jesus to heal you?

# MARCH 12, 2024

**Tuesday of the Fourth Week of Lent**

### John 5:1–16

There was a feast of the Jews, and Jesus went up to Jerusalem. Now there is in Jerusalem at the Sheep Gate a pool called in Hebrew Bethesda, with five porticoes. In these lay a large number of ill, blind, lame, and crippled. One man was there who had been ill for thirty-eight years. When Jesus saw him lying there and knew that he had been ill for a long time, he said to him, "Do you want to be well?" The sick man answered him, "Sir, I have no one to put me into the pool when the water is stirred up; while I am on my way, someone else gets down there before me." Jesus said to him, "Rise, take up your mat, and walk." Immediately the man became well, took up his mat, and walked.

Now that day was a sabbath. So the Jews said to the man who was cured, "It is the sabbath, and it is not lawful for you to carry your mat." He answered them, "The man who made me well told me, 'Take up your mat and walk.'" They asked him, "Who is the man who told you, 'Take it up and walk'?" The man who was healed did not know who it was, for Jesus had

> slipped away, since there was a crowd there. After this Jesus found him in the temple area and said to him, "Look, you are well; do not sin any more, so that nothing worse may happen to you." The man went and told the Jews that Jesus was the one who had made him well. Therefore, the Jews began to persecute Jesus because he did this on a sabbath.

Friends, in today's Gospel, we find the beautiful healing of a paralyzed man who had been ill for thirty-eight years. Jesus sees the man lying on his mat, next to a pool, and asks, "Do you want to be well?" The man says yes, and Jesus replies, "Rise, take up your mat, and walk." Immediately, the man is healed.

Now at this point, the story really heats up. We notice something that is frequently on display in the Gospels: the resistance to the creative work of God, the attempt to find any excuse, however lame, to deny it, to pretend it's not there, to condemn it.

One would expect that everyone around the cured man would rejoice, but just the contrary: the Jewish leaders are infuriated and confounded. They see the healed man, and their first response is, "It is the Sabbath, and it is not lawful for you to carry your mat."

Why are they so reactive? Why don't they want this to be? We sinners don't like the ways of God. We find them troubling and threatening. Why? Because they undermine the games of oppression and exclusion that we rely upon in order to boost our own egos.

Let this encounter remind us that God's ways are not our ways, and that there is one even greater than the sabbath.

**Reflect:** What did the Jewish leaders focus on, and what did they miss or refuse to see? What blinded them?

# MARCH 13, 2024

**Wednesday of the Fourth Week of Lent**

### John 5:17–30

Jesus answered the Jews: "My Father is at work until now, so I am at work." For this reason they tried all the more to kill him, because he not only broke the sabbath but he also called God his own father, making himself equal to God.

Jesus answered and said to them, "Amen, amen, I say to you, the Son cannot do anything on his own, but only what he sees the Father doing; for what he does, the Son will do also. For the Father loves the Son and shows him everything that he himself does, and he will show him greater works than these, so that you may be amazed. For just as the Father raises the dead and gives life, so also does the Son give life to whomever he wishes. Nor does the Father judge anyone, but he has given all judgment to the Son, so that all may honor the Son just as they honor the Father. Whoever does not honor the Son does not honor the Father who sent him. Amen, amen, I say to you, whoever hears my word and believes in the one who sent me has eternal life and will not come to condemnation, but has passed from death to life. Amen, amen, I say to you, the hour is coming and is now here when the dead will hear the voice of the Son of God, and those who hear will live. For just as the Father has life in himself, so also he gave to the Son the possession of life in himself. And he gave him power to exercise judgment, because he is the Son of Man. Do not be amazed at this, because the hour is coming in which all who are in the tombs will hear his voice and will come out, those who have done good deeds to the resurrection of life, but those who have done wicked deeds to the resurrection of condemnation.

"I cannot do anything on my own; I judge as I hear, and my judgment is just, because I do not seek my own will but the will of the one who sent me."

Friends, in today's Gospel, we see Jesus as the judge who shows mercy and love. It is hard to read any two pages of the Bible— Old Testament or New—and not find the language of divine judgment.

Think of judgment as a sort of light, which reveals both the positive and the negative. Beautiful things look even more beautiful when the light shines on them; ugly things look even uglier when they come into the light. When the divine light shines, when judgment takes place, something like real love is unleashed.

Someone might avoid seeing the doctor for years, fearful that he will uncover something diseased or deadly. But how much better it is for you when you do, even when the doctor pronounces a harsh "judgment" on your physical condition!

And this is why judgment is the proper activity of a king. It is not the exercise of arbitrary power, but rather an exercise of real love.

**Reflect:** What do you do to move out of the convenient darkness and shed the light of Christ on your own attitudes and behaviors?

_____

_____

_____

_____

_____

_____

_____

_____

_____

_____

# MARCH 14, 2024

### Thursday of the Fourth Week of Lent

### John 5:31–47

Jesus said to the Jews: "If I testify on my own behalf, my testimony is not true. But there is another who testifies on my behalf, and I know that the testimony he gives on my behalf is true. You sent emissaries to John, and he testified to the truth. I do not accept human testimony, but I say this so that you may be saved. He was a burning and shining lamp, and for a while you were content to rejoice in his light. But I have testimony greater than John's. The works that the Father gave me to accomplish, these works that I perform testify on my behalf that the Father has sent me. Moreover, the Father who sent me has testified on my behalf. But you have never heard his voice nor seen his form, and you do not have his word remaining in you, because you do not believe in the one whom he has sent. You search the Scriptures, because you think you have eternal life through them; even they testify on my behalf. But you do not want to come to me to have life.

"I do not accept human praise; moreover, I know that you do not have the love of God in you. I came in the name of my Father, but you do not accept me; yet if another comes in his own name, you will accept him. How can you believe, when you accept praise from one another and do not seek the praise that comes from the only God? Do not think that I will accuse you before the Father: the one who will accuse you is Moses, in whom you have placed your hope. For if you had believed Moses, you would have believed me, because he wrote about me. But if you do not believe his writings, how will you believe my words?"

Friends, in today's Gospel, Jesus establishes his authority for his words and actions.

You will recall that when at the outset of his ministry the Lord spoke in the synagogue at Capernaum, what first got the attention of the crowd was not what he said but the manner in which he said it. What did they notice? "The people were astonished at his teaching, for he taught them as one having authority and not as the scribes."

We might miss this, but the relevant point is that rabbis and scribes taught through appeal to authorities beyond themselves, ultimately to the authority of Moses. But Jesus did not speak in this manner; rather, he spoke with *exousia* (authority).

What is being implied is that the Word, which spoke to Moses, and through Moses to every other teacher in Israel, is now speaking on his own authority. Don't believe those who say that the divinity of Jesus is affirmed only in the prologue of the Gospel of John. This passage is, for a Jewish audience, just as clear an affirmation of Jesus' divinity as John's "the Word became flesh and made his dwelling among us."

**Reflect:** In this Gospel passage, Jesus says that his works testify on his behalf that he was sent from the Father. How do your works testify that you are sent by Jesus on mission?

_____

_____

_____

_____

_____

_____

_____

_____

_____

_____

_____

_____

# MARCH 15, 2024

### Friday of the Fourth Week of Lent

#### John 7:1–2, 10, 25–30

Jesus moved about within Galilee; he did not wish to travel in Judea, because the Jews were trying to kill him. But the Jewish feast of Tabernacles was near.

But when his brothers had gone up to the feast, he himself also went up, not openly but as it were in secret.

Some of the inhabitants of Jerusalem said, "Is he not the one they are trying to kill? And look, he is speaking openly and they say nothing to him. Could the authorities have realized that he is the Christ? But we know where he is from. When the Christ comes, no one will know where he is from." So Jesus cried out in the temple area as he was teaching and said, "You know me and also know where I am from. Yet I did not come on my own, but the one who sent me, whom you do not know, is true. I know him, because I am from him, and he sent me." So they tried to arrest him, but no one laid a hand upon him, because his hour had not yet come.

Friends, in today's Gospel, Jesus proclaims during the feast of Tabernacles that the Father has sent him.

In his passion to set right a disjointed universe, God broke open his own heart in love. The Father sent into the dysfunction of the world, not simply a representative, spokesman, or plenipotentiary, but his own Son, so that he might gather that world into the bliss of the divine life.

God's center—the love between the Father and the Son—is now offered as our center; God's heart breaks open so as to include even the worst and most hopeless among us. In so many spiritual traditions, the emphasis is placed on the human quest for God, but this is reversed in Christianity.

Christians do not believe that God is dumbly "out there," like a mountain waiting to be climbed by various religious searchers. On the contrary, God, the hound of heaven in Francis Thompson's poem, comes relentlessly searching after us.

Because of this questing and self-emptying divine love, we become friends of God, sharers in the communion of the Trinity. That is the essence of Christianity; everything else is commentary.

**Reflect:** How does God come relentlessly searching for you during your life?

_____

_____

_____

# MARCH 16, 2024

**Saturday of the Fourth Week of Lent**

### John 7:40–53

Some in the crowd who heard these words of Jesus said, "This is truly the Prophet." Others said, "This is the Christ." But others said, "The Christ will not come from Galilee, will he? Does not Scripture say that the Christ will be of David's family and come from Bethlehem, the village where David lived?" So a division occurred in the crowd because of him. Some of them even wanted to arrest him, but no one laid hands on him.

So the guards went to the chief priests and Pharisees, who asked them, "Why did you not bring him?" The guards answered, "Never before has anyone spoken like this man." So the Pharisees answered them, "Have you also been deceived? Have any of the authorities or the Pharisees believed in him? But this crowd, which does not know the law, is accursed." Nicodemus, one of their members who had come to him earlier, said to them, "Does our law condemn a man before it first hears him and finds out what he is doing?" They answered and said to him, "You are not from Galilee also, are you? Look and see that no prophet arises from Galilee."

Then each went to his own house.

Friends, today's Gospel reports the mixed reactions of people to Jesus' message. What does he say as he preaches? "Repent, for the kingdom of heaven is at hand." We mustn't flatten this out or render it too spiritually abstract, as though he were talking only about becoming nicer people, more generous and more kind. His preaching was about more than that. It was part and parcel of his messianic vocation.

What he was saying was something like this: a new order is breaking out in Israel, the tribes are coming back together, and Yahweh is going to reign. Therefore, adjust your lives, your vision, your expectations. Start living even now as members of this new kingdom.

Israelites knew that a major task of the Messiah was to engage the enemies of Israel, to deal definitively with those powers opposed to God's creative purpose. This very much included political oppressors, religious charlatans, and self-absorbed Pharisees—all of whom Jesus deals with and confronts.

**Reflect:** In what ways do you need to repent or to adjust your life, your vision, and your expectations?

_____

_____

_____

_____

_____

# MARCH 17, 2024

### Fifth Sunday of Lent

### John 12:20–33

Some Greeks who had come to worship at the Passover Feast came to Philip, who was from Bethsaida in Galilee, and asked him, "Sir, we would like to see Jesus." Philip went and told Andrew; then Andrew and Philip went and told Jesus. Jesus answered them, "The hour has come for the Son of Man to be glorified. Amen, amen, I say to you, unless a grain of wheat falls to the ground and dies, it remains just a grain of wheat; but if it dies, it produces much fruit. Whoever loves his life loses it, and whoever hates his life in this world will preserve it for eternal life. Whoever serves me must follow me, and where I am, there also will my servant be. The Father will honor whoever serves me.

"I am troubled now. Yet what should I say? 'Father, save me from this hour'? But it was for this purpose that I came to this hour. Father, glorify your name." Then a voice came from heaven, "I have glorified it and will glorify it again." The crowd there heard it and said it was thunder; but others said, "An angel has spoken to him." Jesus answered and said, "This voice did not come for my sake but for yours. Now is the time of judgment on this world; now the ruler of this world will be driven out. And when I am lifted up from the earth, I will draw everyone to myself." He said this indicating the kind of death he would die.

Friends, our Gospel for today contains one of the most beautiful and terrible summations of the Christian message: "Amen, amen, I say to you, unless a grain of wheat falls to the ground and dies, it remains just a grain of wheat; but if it dies, it produces much fruit."

Now this one upon whom the crowds had pinned their hopes is speaking of falling to the earth and dying. And then it gets stranger. "Whoever loves his life loses it, and whoever hates his life in this world will preserve it for life eternal." Come again?!

Just when we are raising you up, you're talking about falling down; just when we are showing you that your life has come to its fulfillment, you're talking about hating this life.

To understand what all this means, we should go back to the grain of wheat that falls to the earth. A seed's life is inside, yes, but it's a life that grows by being given away and mixing with the soil around it. It has to crack open, to be destroyed.

Jesus' sign is the sign of the cross—the death that leads to transfiguration.

**Reflect:** Reflect on the marvel of God's plan of salvation and how he turns suffering into triumph for all who believe.

_____

_____

_____

_____

_____

_____

_____

_____

_____

_____

_____

_____

_____

### John 8:1–11

Jesus went to the Mount of Olives. But early in the morning he arrived again in the temple area, and all the people started coming to him, and he sat down and taught them. Then the scribes and the Pharisees brought a woman who had been caught in adultery and made her stand in the middle. They said to him, "Teacher, this woman was caught in the very act of committing adultery. Now in the law, Moses commanded us to stone such women. So what do you say?" They said this to test him, so that they could have some charge to bring against him. Jesus bent down and began to write on the ground with his finger. But when they continued asking him, he straightened up and said to them, "Let the one among you who is without sin be the first to throw a stone at her." Again he bent down and wrote on the ground. And in response, they went away one by one, beginning with the elders. So he was left alone with the woman before him. Then Jesus straightened up and said to her, "Woman, where are they? Has no one condemned you?" She replied, "No one, sir." Then Jesus said, "Neither do I condemn you. Go, and from now on do not sin any more."

Friends, today's Gospel presents the story of the woman caught in adultery, which is one of the clearest demonstrations of what René Girard called the scapegoat mechanism.

The scribes and Pharisees bring to Jesus a woman they had caught in adultery. Where must they have been standing and how long must they have been waiting in order to catch her? Their eagerness to find a victim is testimony to the insatiable human need for scapegoats.

The novelty of the Gospel is revealed in Jesus' refusal to contribute to the energy of the gathering storm: "Let the one among you who is without sin be the first to throw a stone at her." Jesus directs the energy of scapegoating violence back toward the accusers. He unveils the dangerous secret that the unstable order of the society has been predicated upon scapegoating. The Church Fathers emphasized this point with a neat interpretive move: they imagined that Jesus was writing in the sand none other than the sins of those who were threatening the woman.

Then we see, at least in seminal form, the new order: "Go, and from now on do not sin any more." The connection between Jesus and the woman is not the consequence of condemnation but rather the fruit of forgiveness offered and accepted.

**Reflect:** Consider the prevalence of scapegoating in contemporary culture. Think especially about the times when you have been guilty of singling out an individual or group as a scapegoat.

# MARCH 19, 2024

*Solemnity of Saint Joseph, Spouse of the Blessed Virgin Mary*

**Matthew 1:16, 18–21, 24a (or Luke 2:41–51a)**

Jacob was the father of Joseph, the husband of Mary. Of her was born Jesus who is called the Christ.

Now this is how the birth of Jesus Christ came about. When his mother Mary was betrothed to Joseph, but before they lived together, she was found with child through the Holy Spirit. Joseph her husband, since he was a righteous man, yet unwilling to expose her to shame, decided to divorce her quietly. Such was his intention when, behold, the angel of the Lord appeared to him in a dream and said, "Joseph, son of David, do not be afraid to take Mary your wife into your home. For it is through the Holy Spirit that this child has been conceived in her. She will bear a son and you are to name him Jesus, because he will save his people from their sins." When Joseph awoke, he did as the angel of the Lord had commanded him and took his wife into his home.

Friends, today we celebrate the feast of St. Joseph.

Every episode of Joseph's life is a crisis. He discovered that the woman to whom he was betrothed was pregnant. He resolved to divorce her quietly, but then the angel of the Lord appeared in a dream and explained the anomalous pregnancy. So Joseph understood what was happening in the context of God's providence and took Mary as his wife.

Next, discovering that the child was in mortal danger, Joseph took mother and baby on a perilous journey to an unknown country. Anyone who has ever been forced to move to a new city knows something of the anxiety that Joseph must have felt. But Joseph went because God had commanded him.

Finally, we hear of Joseph desperately seeking his lost twelve-year-old son. Quietly taking the child home, Joseph once more put aside his human feelings and trusted in the purposes of God.

The little we know about Joseph is that he experienced heartbreak, fear unto death, and a parent's deepest anxiety. But each time, he read what happened to him as a theo-drama, not an ego-drama. This shift in attitude is what made Joseph the patron of the universal Church.

**Reflect:** Think of the last crisis you encountered. Did you read it as part of a theo-drama (God's plans and purposes) or as part of an ego-drama (your own plans and purposes)?

# MARCH 20, 2024

## Wednesday of the Fifth Week of Lent

### John 8:31–42

Jesus said to those Jews who believed in him, "If you remain in my word, you will truly be my disciples, and you will know the truth, and the truth will set you free." They answered him, "We are descendants of Abraham and have never been enslaved to anyone. How can you say, 'You will become free'?" Jesus answered them, "Amen, amen, I say to you, everyone who commits sin is a slave of sin. A slave does not remain in a household forever, but a son always remains. So if the Son frees you, then you will truly be free. I know that you are descendants of Abraham. But you are trying to kill me, because my word has no room among you. I tell you what I have seen in the Father's presence; then do what you have heard from the Father."

They answered and said to him, "Our father is Abraham." Jesus said to them, "If you were Abraham's children, you would be doing the works of Abraham. But now you are trying to kill me, a man who has told you the truth that I heard from God; Abraham did not do this. You are doing the works

> of your father!" So they said to him, "We were not born of fornication. We have one Father, God." Jesus said to them, "If God were your Father, you would love me, for I came from God and am here; I did not come on my own, but he sent me."

Friends, in today's Gospel, the Lord tells some Jewish listeners that they are enslaved to sin and that the truth will set them free.

Jesus was distinguishing between *sin* and sins, between the underlying disease and its many symptoms. When the Curé d'Ars was asked what wisdom he had gained about human nature from his many years of hearing confessions, he responded, "People are much sadder than they seem." Blaise Pascal rests his apologetic for Christianity on the simple fact that all people are unhappy. This universal, enduring, and stubborn sadness is sin.

Now, this does not mean that sin is identical to psychological depression. The worst sinners can be the most psychologically well-adjusted people, and the greatest saints can be, by any ordinary measure, quite unhappy.

When I speak of sadness in this context, I mean the deep sense of unfulfillment. We want the truth, and we get it, if at all, in dribs and drabs; we want the good, and we achieve it only rarely; we seem to know what we ought to be, but we are in fact something else. This spiritual frustration, this inner warfare, this debility of soul, is sin.

**Reflect:** We are all tainted by the "underlying disease" of sin. What is the connection between our fallen human nature and your own unhappiness or unfulfillment?

_____

_____

_____

_____

_____

_____

_____

_____

_____

_____

_____

_____

_____

_____

# MARCH 21, 2024

**Thursday of the Fifth Week of Lent**

### John 8:51–59

Jesus said to the Jews: "Amen, amen, I say to you, whoever keeps my word will never see death." So the Jews said to him, "Now we are sure that you are possessed. Abraham died, as did the prophets, yet you say, 'Whoever keeps my word will never taste death.' Are you greater than our father Abraham, who died? Or the prophets, who died? Who do you make yourself out to be?" Jesus answered, "If I glorify myself, my glory is worth nothing; but it is my Father who glorifies me, of whom you say, 'He is our God.' You do not know him, but I know him. And if I should say that I do not know him, I would be like you a liar. But I do know him and I keep his word. Abraham your father rejoiced to see my day; he saw it and was glad." So the Jews said to him, "You are not yet fifty years old and you have seen Abraham?" Jesus said to them, "Amen, amen, I say to you, before Abraham came to be, I AM." So they picked up stones to throw at him; but Jesus hid and went out of the temple area.

Friends, in today's Gospel, Jesus asserts his pre-existence by declaring that "before Abraham came to be, I AM."

There has been a disturbing tendency in recent years to turn Jesus into an inspiring spiritual teacher. But if that's all he is, the heck with him. The Gospels are never content with such a reductive description. Though they present him as a teacher, they know that he is infinitely more than that. That something else is at stake in him and our relation to him.

Scripture clearly teaches that Jesus is divine. He once declared, "Have faith in God; have faith also in me." We can easily imagine other religious founders urging faith in God, but we'd be hard pressed to imagine them urging the same faith in themselves! But on Jesus' lips, the two are parallel.

As C.S. Lewis so vividly saw, this means that Jesus compels us to make a choice the way no other figure does. Either you are with Jesus, or you are against him. There is no other way to take in this language. To get this wonderful paradox is to come close to the heart of what it means to be a Christian.

**Reflect:** Reflect on this statement: "Either you are with Jesus, or you are against him." Where do you stand?

_____

_____

_____

_____

_____

# MARCH 22, 2024

### Friday of the Fifth Week of Lent

### John 10:31–42

The Jews picked up rocks to stone Jesus. Jesus answered them, "I have shown you many good works from my Father. For which of these are you trying to stone me?" The Jews answered him, "We are not stoning you for a good work but for blasphemy. You, a man, are making yourself God." Jesus answered them, "Is it not written in your law, 'I said, "You are gods"'? If it calls them gods to whom the word of God came, and Scripture cannot be set aside, can you say that the one whom the Father has consecrated and sent into the world blasphemes because I said, 'I am the Son of God'? If I do not perform my Father's works, do not believe me; but if I perform them, even if you do not believe me, believe the works, so that you may realize and understand that the Father is in me and I am in the Father." Then they tried again to arrest him; but he escaped from their power.

He went back across the Jordan to the place where John first baptized, and there he remained. Many came to him and said, "John performed no sign, but everything John said about this man was true." And many there began to believe in him.

Friends, in today's Gospel, Jesus declares, "The Father is in me and I am in the Father."

Charles Williams stated that the master idea of Christianity is "coinherence," mutual indwelling. If you want to see this idea concretely displayed, look to the pages of the Book of Kells, that masterpiece of early Christian illumination. Lines interwoven, designs turning in and around on each other, plays of plants, animals, planets, human beings, angels, and saints. The Germans call it *Ineinander* (one in the other).

How do we identify ourselves? Almost exclusively through the naming of relationships: we are sons, brothers, daughters, sisters, mothers, fathers, members of organizations, members of the Church, etc. We might want to be alone, but no one and nothing is finally an island. Coinherence is indeed the name of the game, at all levels of reality.

And God—the ultimate reality—is a family of coinherent relations, each marked by the capacity for self-emptying. Though Father and Son are really distinct, they are utterly implicated in each other by a mutual act of love.

The impossibly good news is that Jesus and the Father have invited us to enter fully into their divine coinherence. The love between the Father and the Son—which is called "the Holy Spirit"—can be participated in.

**Reflect:** What is the difference between following God and participating in his divine life?

# MARCH 23, 2024

### Saturday of the Fifth Week of Lent

### John 11:45–56

Many of the Jews who had come to Mary and seen what Jesus had done began to believe in him. But some of them went to the Pharisees and told them what Jesus had done. So the chief priests and the Pharisees convened the Sanhedrin and said, "What are we going to do? This man is performing many signs. If we leave him alone, all will believe in him, and the Romans will come and take away both our land and our nation." But one of them, Caiaphas, who was high priest that year, said to them, "You know nothing, nor do you consider that it is better for you that one man should die instead of the people, so that the whole nation may not perish." He did not say this on his own, but since he was high priest for that year, he prophesied that Jesus was going to die for the nation, and not only for the nation, but also to gather into one the dispersed children of God. So from that day on they planned to kill him.

So Jesus no longer walked about in public among the Jews, but he left for the region near the desert, to a

> town called Ephraim, and there he remained with his disciples.
>
> Now the Passover of the Jews was near, and many went up from the country to Jerusalem before Passover to purify themselves. They looked for Jesus and said to one another as they were in the temple area, "What do you think? That he will not come to the feast?"

Friends, in today's Gospel, the chief priests and Pharisees unite in a plot to kill Jesus because he raised Lazarus from the dead.

The Crucifixion of Jesus is a classic instance of Catholic philosopher René Girard's scapegoating theory. He held that a society, large or small, that finds itself in conflict comes together through a common act of blaming an individual or group purportedly responsible for the conflict.

It is utterly consistent with the Girardian theory that Caiaphas, the leading religious figure of the time, said to his colleagues, "It is better for you that one man should die instead of the people, so that the whole nation may not perish."

In any other religious context, this sort of rationalization would be validated. But in the Resurrection of Jesus from the dead, this stunning truth is revealed: God is not on the side of the scapegoaters, but rather on the side of the scapegoated victim.

The true God does not sanction a community created through violence; rather, he sanctions what Jesus called the kingdom of God, a society grounded in forgiveness, love, and identification with the victim.

**Reflect:** How did the Resurrection invalidate the scapegoating that Caiaphas supported?

### Mark 15:1–39 (short version)

As soon as morning came, the chief priests with the elders and the scribes, that is, the whole Sanhedrin, held a council. They bound Jesus, led him away, and handed him over to Pilate. Pilate questioned him, "Are you the king of the Jews?" He said to him in reply, "You say so." The chief priests accused him of many things. Again Pilate questioned him, "Have you no answer? See how many things they accuse you of." Jesus gave him no further answer, so that Pilate was amazed.

Now on the occasion of the feast he used to release to them one prisoner whom they requested. A man called Barabbas was then in prison along with the rebels who had committed murder in a rebellion. The crowd came forward and began to ask him to do for them as he was accustomed. Pilate answered, "Do you want me to release to you the king of the Jews?" For he knew that it was out of envy that the chief priests had handed him over. But the chief priests stirred up the crowd to have him release Barabbas for them instead. Pilate again said to them in reply, "Then what do you want me to do with the man you call the king of the Jews?" They shouted again, "Crucify him." Pilate said to them, "Why? What evil has he done?" They only shouted the louder, "Crucify him." So Pilate, wishing to satisfy the crowd, released Barabbas to them and, after he had Jesus scourged, handed him over to be crucified.

The soldiers led him away inside the palace, that is, the praetorium, and assembled the whole cohort. They clothed him in purple and, weaving a crown of thorns, placed it on him. They began to salute him with, "Hail, King of the Jews!" and kept striking his head with a reed and spitting upon him. They knelt before him in homage. And when they had mocked him, they stripped him of the purple cloak, dressed him in his own clothes, and led him out to crucify him.

They pressed into service a passer-by, Simon, a Cyrenian, who was coming in from the country, the father of Alexander and Rufus, to carry his cross.

They brought him to the place of Golgotha—which is translated Place of the Skull. They gave him wine drugged with myrrh, but he did not take it. Then they crucified him and divided his garments by casting lots for them to see what each should take. It was nine o'clock in the morning when they crucified him. The inscription of the charge against him read,

"The King of the Jews." With him they crucified two revolutionaries, one on his right and one on his left. Those passing by reviled him, shaking their heads and saying, "Aha! You who would destroy the temple and rebuild it in three days, save yourself by coming down from the cross." Likewise the chief priests, with the scribes, mocked him among themselves and said, "He saved others; he cannot save himself. Let the Christ, the King of Israel, come down now from the cross that we may see and believe." Those who were crucified with him also kept abusing him.

At noon darkness came over the whole land until three in the afternoon. And at three o'clock Jesus cried out in a loud voice, "*Eloi, Eloi, lema sabachthani?*" which is translated, "My God, my God, why have you forsaken me?" Some of the bystanders who heard it said, "Look, he is calling Elijah." One of them ran, soaked a sponge with wine, put it on a reed and gave it to him to drink saying, "Wait, let us see if Elijah comes to take him down." Jesus gave a loud cry and breathed his last.

*Here all kneel and pause for a short time.*

The veil of the sanctuary was torn in two from top to bottom. When the centurion who stood facing him saw how he breathed his last he said, "Truly this man was the Son of God!"

Friends, on this Palm Sunday, we are privileged to become immersed in Mark's great Passion narrative, where the kingship of Jesus emerges with great clarity—and also with great irony.

We read that upon being brought before the Sanhedrin, Jesus is asked whether he is the Messiah, an implicit reference to David. When Jesus calmly responds, "I am," the high priest tears his robes, for how could a shackled criminal possibly be the kingly descendant of David? Upon being presented to Pilate, Jesus is asked the functionally equivalent question: "Are you the king of the Jews?" Again a calmly affirmative answer comes: "You say so." This leads the soldiers to mock him, placing a purple cloak on his shoulders and a crown of thorns on his head.

Mark does not want us to miss the irony that, precisely as the King of the Jews and the Son of David, Jesus is implicitly king to those soldiers. For the mission of the Davidic king is the unification not only of the tribes of Israel but also of the tribes of the world. What commenced with David's gathering of the tribes of Israel would soon reach completion in the criminal raised high on the cross, thereby drawing all people to himself.

**Reflect:** How is Jesus king of your life right now? How can you support the building of his everlasting kingdom?

_____

_____

_____

_____

# MARCH 25, 2024

**Monday of Holy Week**

### John 12:1–11

Six days before Passover Jesus came to Bethany, where Lazarus was, whom Jesus had raised from the dead. They gave a dinner for him there, and Martha served, while Lazarus was one of those reclining at table with him. Mary took a liter of costly perfumed oil made from genuine aromatic nard and anointed the feet of Jesus and dried them with her hair; the house was filled with the fragrance of the oil. Then Judas the Iscariot, one of his disciples, and the one who would betray him, said, "Why was this oil not sold for three hundred days' wages and given to the poor?" He said this not because he cared about the poor but because he was a thief and held the money bag and used to steal the contributions. So Jesus said, "Leave her alone. Let her keep this for the day of my burial. You always have the poor with you, but you do not always have me."

The large crowd of the Jews found out that he was there and came, not only because of him, but also to see Lazarus, whom he had raised from the dead. And the chief priests plotted to kill Lazarus too, because many of the Jews were turning away and believing in Jesus because of him.

Friends, in today's Gospel, Mary of Bethany anoints Jesus' feet with perfumed oil, preparing him for burial.

This gesture—wasting something as expensive as an entire jar of perfume—is sniffed at by Judas, who complains that, at the very least, the nard could have been sold and the money given to the poor.

Why does John use this tale to preface his telling of the Passion? Why does he allow the odor of this woman's perfume to waft, as it were, over the whole of the story? It is because, I believe, this extravagant gesture shows forth the meaning of what Jesus is about to do: the absolutely radical giving away of self.

There is nothing calculating, careful, or conservative about the woman's action. Flowing from the deepest place in the heart, religion resists the strictures set for it by a fussily moralizing reason (on full display in those who complain about the woman's extravagance). At the climax of his life, Jesus will give himself away totally, lavishly, unreasonably—and this is why Mary's beautiful gesture is a sort of overture to the opera that will follow.

**Reflect:** When have you been the giver or the recipient of an extravagant gesture of love? How did that affect you?

# MARCH 26, 2024

### Tuesday of Holy Week

### John 13:21–33, 36–38

Reclining at table with his disciples, Jesus was deeply troubled and testified, "Amen, amen, I say to you, one of you will betray me." The disciples looked at one another, at a loss as to whom he meant. One of his disciples, the one whom Jesus loved, was reclining at Jesus' side. So Simon Peter nodded to him to find out whom he meant. He leaned back against Jesus' chest and said to him, "Master, who is it?" Jesus answered, "It is the one to whom I hand the morsel after I have dipped it." So he dipped the morsel and took it and handed it to Judas, son of Simon the Iscariot. After Judas took the morsel, Satan entered him. So Jesus said to him, "What you are going to do, do quickly." Now none of those reclining at table realized why he said this to him. Some thought that since Judas kept the money bag, Jesus had told him, "Buy what we need for the feast," or to give something to the poor. So Judas took the morsel and left at once. And it was night.

When he had left, Jesus said, "Now is the Son of Man glorified, and God is glorified in him. If God is glorified in him, God will also glorify him in himself, and he will glorify him at once. My children, I will be with you only a little while longer. You will look for me, and as I told the Jews, 'Where I go you cannot come,' so now I say it to you."

Simon Peter said to him, "Master, where are you going?" Jesus answered him, "Where I am going, you cannot follow me now, though you will follow later." Peter said to him, "Master, why can I not follow you now? I will lay down my life for you." Jesus answered, "Will you lay down your life for me? Amen, amen, I say to you, the cock will not crow before you deny me three times."

Friends, today's Gospel is from John's account of the Last Supper, where Jesus acknowledges Judas as his betrayer and tells him to get on with it.

God's desires have been, from the beginning, opposed. Consistently, human beings have preferred the isolation of sin to the festivity of the sacred meal. Theologians have called this anomalous tendency the *mysterium iniquitatis* (the mystery of iniquity), for there is no rational ground for it, no reason for it to exist.

But there it stubbornly is, always shadowing the good, parasitic upon that which it tries to destroy. Therefore, we should not be too surprised that, as the sacred meal comes to its richest possible expression, evil accompanies it.

Judas the betrayer expresses the *mysterium iniquitatis* with particular symbolic power, for he had spent years in intimacy with Jesus, taking in the Lord's moves and thoughts at close quarters, sharing the table of fellowship with him—and yet he saw fit to turn Jesus over to his enemies and to interrupt the coinherence of the Last Supper.

Those of us who regularly gather around the table of intimacy with Christ and yet engage consistently in the works of darkness are meant to see ourselves in the betrayer.

**Reflect:** When have you been confronted with the "mystery of evil," and what role did your faith play in processing that confrontation?

### Matthew 26:14–25

One of the Twelve, who was called Judas Iscariot, went to the chief priests and said, "What are you willing to give me if I hand him over to you?" They paid him thirty pieces of silver, and from that time on he looked for an opportunity to hand him over.

On the first day of the Feast of Unleavened Bread, the disciples approached Jesus and said, "Where do you want us to prepare for you to eat the Passover?" He said, "Go into the city to a certain man and tell him, 'The teacher says, My appointed time draws near; in your house I shall celebrate the Passover with my disciples.'" The disciples then did as Jesus had ordered, and prepared the Passover.

When it was evening, he reclined at table with the Twelve. And while they were eating, he said, "Amen, I say to you, one of you will betray me." Deeply distressed at this, they began to say to him one after another, "Surely it is not I, Lord?" He said in reply, "He who has dipped his hand into the dish with me is the one who will betray me. The Son of Man indeed goes, as it is written of him, but woe to that man by whom the Son of Man is betrayed. It would be better for that man if he had never been born." Then Judas, his betrayer, said in reply, "Surely it is not I, Rabbi?" He answered, "You have said so."

Friends, in today's Gospel, Jesus asks his disciples to go into Jerusalem and prepare a Passover supper.

At the heart of the Passover meal was the eating of a lamb, which had been sacrificed, in remembrance of the lambs of the original Passover, whose blood had been smeared on the doorposts of the Israelites in Egypt. Making his Last Supper a Passover meal, Jesus was signaling the fulfillment of John the Baptist's prophecy that he, Jesus, would be the Lamb of God and the definitive sacrifice.

This sacrifice is made sacramentally present at every Mass—not for the sake of God, who has no need of it, but for our sake. In the Mass, we participate in the act by which divinity and humanity are reconciled, and we eat the sacrificed body and drink the poured-out blood of the Lamb of God.

**Reflect:** How does partaking in the Body and Blood of Jesus at Mass affect you?

# MARCH 28, 2024

*Thursday of the Lord's Supper*

### John 13:1–15

Before the feast of Passover, Jesus knew that his hour had come to pass from this world to the Father. He loved his own in the world and he loved them to the end. The devil had already induced Judas, son of Simon the Iscariot, to hand him over. So, during supper, fully aware that the Father had put everything into his power and that he had come from God and was returning to God, he rose from supper and took off his outer garments. He took a towel and tied it around his waist. Then he poured water into a basin and began to wash the disciples' feet and dry them with the towel around his waist. He came to Simon Peter, who said to him, "Master, are you going to wash my feet?" Jesus answered and said to him, "What I am doing, you do not understand now, but you will understand later." Peter said to him, "You will never wash my feet." Jesus answered him, "Unless I wash you, you will have no inheritance with me." Simon Peter said to him, "Master, then not only my feet, but my hands and head as well." Jesus said to him, "Whoever has bathed has no need except to have his feet washed, for he is clean all over; so you are clean, but not all." For he knew who would betray him; for this reason, he said, "Not all of you are clean."

So when he had washed their feet and put his garments back on and reclined at table again, he said to them, "Do you realize what I have done for you? You call me 'teacher' and 'master,' and rightly so, for indeed I am. If I, therefore, the master and teacher, have washed your feet, you ought to wash one another's feet. I have given you a model to follow, so that as I have done for you, you should also do."

Friends, in today's Gospel, Jesus washes the disciples' feet. He is giving them a visual proclamation of his new commandment: "Love one another. As I have loved you, so you also should love one another."

When we accept this commandment, we walk the path of joy. When we internalize this law, we become happy. And so the paradox: happiness is never a function of filling oneself up; it is a wonderful function of giving oneself away.

When the divine grace enters one's life (and everything we have is the result of divine grace), the task is to contrive a way to make it a gift. In a sense, the divine life—which exists only in gift form—can be "had" only on the fly.

Notice please that we are to love with a properly divine love: "I have called you friends, because I have told you everything I have heard from my Father." Radical, radical, radical. Complete, excessive, over-the-top.

**Reflect:** How can you practice this radical love in a concrete way today?

_____

_____

_____

_____

_____

_____

_____

_____

_____

_____

_____

# MARCH 29, 2024

*Friday of the Passion of the Lord (Good Friday)*

### John 18:1–19:42

Jesus went out with his disciples across the Kidron valley to where there was a garden, into which he and his disciples entered. Judas his betrayer also knew the place, because Jesus had often met there with his disciples. So Judas got a band of soldiers and guards from the chief priests and the Pharisees and went there with lanterns, torches, and weapons. Jesus, knowing everything that was going to happen to him, went out and said to them, "Whom are you looking for?" They answered him, "Jesus the Nazorean." He said to them, "I AM." Judas his betrayer was also with them. When he said to them, "I AM," they turned away and fell to the ground. So he again asked them, "Whom are you looking for?" They said, "Jesus the Nazorean." Jesus answered, "I told you that I AM. So if you are looking for me, let these men go." This was to fulfill what he had said, "I have not lost any of those you gave me." Then Simon Peter, who had a sword, drew it, struck the high priest's slave, and cut off his right ear. The slave's name was Malchus. Jesus said to Peter, "Put your sword into its scabbard. Shall I not drink the cup that the Father gave me?"

So the band of soldiers, the tribune, and the Jewish guards seized Jesus, bound him, and brought him to Annas first. He was the father-in-law of Caiaphas, who was high priest that year. It was Caiaphas who had counseled the Jews that it was better that one man should die rather than the people.

Simon Peter and another disciple followed Jesus. Now the other disciple was known to the high priest, and he entered the courtyard of the high priest with Jesus. But Peter stood at the gate outside. So the other disciple, the acquaintance of the high priest, went out and spoke to the gatekeeper and brought Peter in. Then the maid who was the gatekeeper said to Peter, "You are not one of this man's disciples, are you?" He said, "I am not." Now the slaves and the guards were standing around a charcoal fire that they had made, because it was cold, and were warming themselves. Peter was also standing there keeping warm.

The high priest questioned Jesus about his disciples and about his doctrine. Jesus answered him, "I have spoken publicly to the world. I have always taught in a synagogue or in the temple area where all the Jews gather, and in secret I have said nothing. Why ask me? Ask those who heard me what I said to them. They know what I said." When he had said this, one of the temple guards standing there struck Jesus and said, "Is this the way you answer the high priest?" Jesus answered him, "If I have spoken wrongly, testify to the wrong; but if I have spoken rightly, why do you strike me?" Then Annas sent him bound to Caiaphas the high priest.

Now Simon Peter was standing there keeping warm. And they said to him, "You are not one of his disciples, are you?" He denied it and said, "I am not." One of the slaves of the high priest, a relative of the one whose ear Peter had cut off, said, "Didn't I see you in the garden with him?" Again Peter denied it. And immediately the cock crowed.

Then they brought Jesus from Caiaphas to the praetorium. It was morning. And they themselves did not enter the praetorium, in order not to be defiled so that they could eat the Passover. So Pilate came out to them and said, "What charge do you bring against this man?" They answered and said to him, "If he were not a criminal, we would not have handed him over to you." At this, Pilate said to them, "Take him yourselves, and judge him according to your law." The Jews answered him, "We do not have the right to execute anyone," in order that the word of Jesus might be fulfilled that he said indicating the kind of death he would die. So Pilate went back into the praetorium and summoned Jesus and said to him, "Are you the King of the Jews?" Jesus answered, "Do you say this on your own or have others told you about me?" Pilate answered, "I am not a Jew, am I? Your own nation and the chief priests handed you over to me. What have you done?" Jesus answered, "My kingdom does not belong to this world. If my kingdom did belong to this world, my attendants would be fighting to keep me from being handed over to the Jews. But as it is, my kingdom is not here." So Pilate said to him, "Then you are a king?" Jesus answered, "You say I am a king. For this I was born and for this I came into the world, to testify to the truth. Everyone who belongs to the truth listens to my voice." Pilate said to him, "What is truth?"

When he had said this, he again went out to the Jews and said to them, "I find no guilt in him. But you have a custom that I release one prisoner to you at Passover. Do you want me to release to you the King of the Jews?" They cried out again, "Not this one but Barabbas!" Now Barabbas was a revolutionary.

Then Pilate took Jesus and had him scourged. And the soldiers wove a crown out of thorns and placed it on his head, and clothed him in a purple cloak, and they came to him and said, "Hail, King of the Jews!" And they struck him repeatedly. Once more Pilate went out and said to them, "Look, I am bringing him out to you, so that you may know that I find no guilt in him." So Jesus came out, wearing the crown of thorns and the purple cloak. And he said to them, "Behold, the man!" When the chief priests and the guards saw him they cried out, "Crucify him, crucify him!" Pilate said to them, "Take him yourselves and crucify him. I find no guilt in him." The Jews answered, "We have a law, and according to that law he ought to die, because he made himself the Son of God." Now when Pilate heard this statement, he became even more afraid, and went back into the praetorium and said to Jesus, "Where are you from?" Jesus did not answer him. So Pilate said to him, "Do you not speak to me? Do you not know that I have power to release you and I have power to crucify you?" Jesus answered him, "You would have no power over me if it had not been given to you from above. For this reason the one who handed me over to you has the greater sin." Consequently, Pilate tried to release him; but the Jews cried out, "If you release him, you are not a Friend of Caesar. Everyone who makes himself a king opposes Caesar."

When Pilate heard these words he brought Jesus out and seated him on the judge's bench in the place called Stone Pavement, in Hebrew, Gabbatha. It was preparation day for Passover, and it was about noon. And he said to the Jews, "Behold, your king!" They cried out, "Take him away, take him away! Crucify him!" Pilate said to them, "Shall I crucify your king?" The chief priests answered, "We have no king but Caesar." Then he handed him over to them to be crucified.

So they took Jesus, and, carrying the cross himself, he went out to what is called the Place of the Skull, in Hebrew, Golgotha. There they crucified him, and with him two others, one on either side, with Jesus in the middle. Pilate also had an inscription written and put on the cross. It read, "Jesus the Nazorean, the King of the Jews." Now many of the Jews read this inscription, because the place where Jesus was crucified was near the city; and it was written in Hebrew, Latin, and Greek. So the chief priests of the Jews said to Pilate, "Do not write 'The King of the Jews,' but that he said, 'I am the King of the Jews.'" Pilate answered, "What I have written, I have written."

When the soldiers had crucified Jesus, they took his clothes and divided them into four shares, a share for each soldier. They also took his tunic, but the tunic was seamless, woven in one piece from the top down. So they said to one another, "Let's not tear it, but cast lots for it to see whose it will be," in order that the passage of Scripture might be fulfilled that says:

> They divided my garments among them,
> and for my vesture they cast lots.

This is what the soldiers did. Standing by the cross of Jesus were his mother and his mother's sister, Mary the wife of Clopas, and Mary of Magdala. When Jesus saw his mother and the disciple there whom he loved he said to his mother, "Woman, behold, your son." Then he said to the disciple, "Behold, your mother." And from that hour the disciple took her into his home.

After this, aware that everything was now finished, in order that the Scripture might be fulfilled, Jesus said, "I thirst." There was a vessel filled with common wine. So they put a sponge soaked in wine on a sprig of hyssop and put it up to his mouth. When Jesus had taken the wine, he said, "It is finished." And bowing his head, he handed over the spirit.

*Here all kneel and pause for a short time.*

Now since it was preparation day, in order that the bodies might not remain on the cross on the sabbath, for the sabbath day of that week was a solemn one, the Jews asked Pilate that their legs be broken and that they be taken down. So the soldiers came and broke the legs of the first and then of the other one who was crucified with Jesus. But when they came to Jesus and saw that he was already dead, they did not break his legs, but one soldier thrust his lance into his side, and immediately blood and water flowed out. An eyewitness has testified, and his testimony is true; he knows that he is speaking the truth, so that you also may come to believe. For this happened so that the Scripture passage might be fulfilled:

*Not a bone of it will be broken.*
And again another passage says:
*They will look upon him whom they have pierced.*

After this, Joseph of Arimathea, secretly a disciple of Jesus for fear of the Jews, asked Pilate if he could remove the body of Jesus. And Pilate permitted it. So he came and took his body. Nicodemus, the one who had first come to him at night, also came bringing a mixture of myrrh and aloes weighing about one hundred pounds. They took the body of Jesus and bound it with burial cloths along with the spices, according to the Jewish burial custom. Now in the place where he had been crucified there was a garden, and in the garden a new tomb, in which no one had yet been buried. So they laid Jesus there because of the Jewish preparation day; for the tomb was close by.

Friends, today's Gospel is John's wonderful narrative of Christ's Passion.

On the cross, Jesus entered into close quarters with sin (because that's where we sinners are found) and allowed the heat and fury of sin to destroy him, even as he protected us.

We can see, with special clarity, why the first Christians associated the crucified Jesus with the suffering servant of Isaiah. By enduring the pain of the cross, Jesus did indeed bear our sins; by his stripes we were indeed healed.

And this is why the sacrificial death of Jesus is pleasing to the Father. The Father sent his Son into godforsakenness, into the morass of sin and death—not because he delighted in seeing his Son suffer, but rather because he wanted his Son to bring the divine light to the darkest place.

It is not the agony of the Son in itself that pleases his Father, but rather the Son's willing obedience in offering his body in sacrifice in order to take away the sin of the world. St. Anselm said that the death of the Son reestablished the right relationship between divinity and humanity.

**Reflect:** Why does the sacrificial death of Jesus on the cross showcase the greatest love?

# MARCH 30, 2024

*Holy Saturday: Easter Vigil*

### Mark 16:1–7

When the sabbath was over, Mary Magdalene, Mary, the mother of James, and Salome bought spices so that they might go and anoint him. Very early when the sun had risen, on the first day of the week, they came to the tomb. They were saying to one another, "Who will roll back the stone for us from the entrance to the tomb?" When they looked up, they saw that the stone had been rolled back; it was very large. On entering the tomb they saw a young man sitting on the right side, clothed in a white robe, and they were utterly amazed. He said to them, "Do not be amazed! You seek Jesus of Nazareth, the crucified. He has been raised; he is not here. Behold the place where they laid him. But go and tell his disciples and Peter, 'He is going before you to Galilee; there you will see him, as he told you.'"

Friends, on this Easter Vigil, in our Gospel we hear St. Mark's account of the Resurrection. The Resurrection of Jesus from the dead is the be-all and end-all of the Christian faith. If Jesus didn't rise from the dead, all bishops, priests, and Christian ministers should go home and get honest jobs, and all the Christian faithful should leave their churches immediately.

As Paul himself put it: "If Christ has not been raised, then empty [too] is our preaching. . . . We are the most pitiable people of all." It's no good, of course, trying to explain the Resurrection away or rationalize it as a myth, a symbol, or an inner subjective experience. None of that does justice to the novelty and sheer strangeness of the biblical message.

It comes down finally to this: if Jesus was not raised from death, Christianity is a fraud and a joke. But if he did rise from death, then Christianity is the fullness of God's revelation, and Jesus must be the absolute center of our lives. There is no third option.

**Reflect:** Why is the Resurrection really the startling "Good News" of the Gospel?

_____

_____

_____

_____

_____

_____

_____

_____

### John 20:1–9

On the first day of the week, Mary of Magdala came to the tomb early in the morning, while it was still dark, and saw the stone removed from the tomb. So she ran and went to Simon Peter and to the other disciple whom Jesus loved, and told them, "They have taken the Lord from the tomb, and we don't know where they put him." So Peter and the other disciple went out and came to the tomb. They both ran, but the other disciple ran faster than Peter and arrived at the tomb first; he bent down and saw the burial cloths there, but did not go in. When Simon Peter arrived after him, he went into the tomb and saw the burial cloths there, and the cloth that had covered his head, not with the burial cloths but rolled up in a separate place. Then the other disciple also went in, the one who had arrived at the tomb first, and he saw and believed. For they did not yet understand the Scripture that he had to rise from the dead.

Friends, our Easter Gospel contains St. John's magnificent account of the Resurrection.

There are three key lessons that follow from the disquieting fact of the Resurrection. First, this world is not all there is. The Resurrection of Jesus from the dead shows as definitively as possible that God is up to something greater than we had imagined. We don't have to live as though death were our master and as though nihilism were the only coherent point of view. We can, in fact, begin to see this world as a place of gestation toward something higher, more permanent, more splendid.

Second, the tyrants know that their time is up. Remember that the cross was Rome's way of asserting its authority. But when Jesus was raised from the dead through the power of the Holy Spirit, the first Christians knew that Caesar's days were, in point of fact, numbered. The faculty lounge interpretation of the Resurrection as a subjective event or a mere symbol is exactly what the tyrants of the world want, for it poses no real threat to them.

Third, the path of salvation has been opened to everyone. Jesus went all the way down, journeying into pain, despair, alienation, even godforsakenness. He went as far as you can go away from the Father. Why? In order to reach all those who had wandered from God. In light of the Resurrection, the first Christians came to know that, even as we run as fast as we can away from the Father, we are running into the arms of the Son.

Let us not domesticate these still-stunning lessons of the Resurrection. Rather, let us allow them to unnerve us, change us, and set us on fire.

**Reflect:** How does the Resurrection imbue your daily life with hope?

# CONCLUSION

Friends,

In the name of the Risen Lord, greetings! Lent is over and we've now moved into Easter. Alleluia!

I'd like to thank you for joining me on this journey through the Lenten season. Now that we've finished, you might be wondering, what's next? How do I maintain the spiritual momentum I developed during Lent? I'd like to suggest a few practical tips.

First, be sure to visit our website, wordonfire.org, on a regular basis. There you'll find lots of helpful resources, including new articles, videos, podcasts, and homilies, all designed to help strengthen your faith and evangelize the culture. The best part is that all of it is free!

In addition to those free resources, I invite you to join our Word on Fire Institute. This is an online hub of deep spiritual and intellectual formation, where you'll journey through courses taught by me and other Fellows. Our goal is to build an army of evangelists, people who have been transformed by Christ and want to bring his light to the world. Learn more and sign up at https://wordonfire.institute.

Finally, consider carrying on your Lenten progress by grounding your life more concretely in the Eucharist, which is what keeps us alive spiritually. Are you only attending Mass on Sundays?

Commit to attending one extra Mass each week. Is there a chapel nearby that offers Eucharistic Adoration? Sign up for a weekly hour of meditation and prayer before the Blessed Sacrament. The Eucharist is the alpha and the omega of Christian discipleship. It is the energy without which authentic Christianity runs down.

Again, thank you from all of us at Word on Fire, and God bless you during this Easter season!

Peace,

+ Robert Barron

Bishop Robert Barron

THE STATIONS OF

# *THE CROSS*

Visit stations.wordonfire.org for
the Stations of the Cross with Bishop Barron.

*All Stations of the Cross images are from the Church
of All Saints in Blato, Korcula Island, Croatia.*

# *OPENING PRAYER*

In the name of the Father, and of the Son,
and of the Holy Spirit.
Amen.

℣. Lord Jesus Christ, Son of God,
℟. Have mercy on me, a sinner.
℣. Lord Jesus Christ, Son of God,
℟. Have mercy on me, a sinner.
℣. Lord Jesus Christ, Son of God,
℟. Have mercy on me, a sinner.

## The First Station
# *JESUS IS CONDEMNED TO DEATH*

℣. We adore you, O Christ, and we bless you. *(Genuflect)*
℟. Because by your holy cross you have redeemed the world. *(Rise)*

**Leader:** Jesus stands before Pontius Pilate, the local representative of Caesar. Pilate, undoubtedly sure of his worldly power and authority, sizes up this criminal, asking, "Are you the King of the Jews?" Jesus responds, "My kingdom does not belong to this world. . . . For this I came into the world, to testify to the truth." Unimpressed, Pilate asks, "What is truth?" And then he condemns Jesus to death. *(Kneel)*

**All pray:** Lord Jesus, Israel dreamed of a new King who would defeat its enemies and reign over the whole world. You accomplished this through your cross and Resurrection, outmaneuvering the sin of the world and swallowing it up in the divine forgiveness. Help us to give our full allegiance to you each day, rejecting the old reign of violence and power and embracing your reign of nonviolence and love.

**(Optional)**

Our Father, who art in heaven,
hallowed be thy name;
thy kingdom come,
thy will be done
on earth as it is in heaven.
Give us this day our daily bread,
and forgive us our trespasses,
as we forgive those who trespass against us;
and lead us not into temptation,
but deliver us from evil.
Amen.

Hail Mary, full of grace, the Lord is with thee;
blessed art thou among women,
and blessed is the fruit of thy womb, Jesus.
Holy Mary, Mother of God,
pray for us sinners,
now and at the hour of our death.
Amen.

Glory be to the Father, and to the Son, and to the Holy
Spirit; as it was in the beginning, is now, and ever shall
be, world without end.
Amen.

*(Rise)*

**All sing:**

*Stabat Mater dolorosa*
*Iuxta Crucem lacrimosa,*
*Dum pendebat Filius.*

At the cross her station keeping,
Stood the mournful Mother weeping,
Close to Jesus to the last.

# *JESUS TAKES UP HIS CROSS*

℣. We adore you, O Christ, and we bless you.
*(Genuflect)*
℟. Because by your holy cross you have redeemed
the world. *(Rise)*

**Leader:** God the Father sends his Son to the
cross—not out of anger, but out of love; not to see
him suffer, but to set things right. "For God so
loved the world that he gave his only Son, so that
everyone who believes in him might not perish but
might have eternal life." God the Son willingly
takes up that terrible cross—a sacrifice expressive of
compassion for us sinners. *(Kneel)*

**All pray:** Lord Jesus, you took up the cross; give us
the grace to take up our cross daily and follow you.
You lived in self-forgetting love unto death; give us
the grace to be such love. You broke open your own
heart for us; give us the grace to open our hearts for
others.

**(Optional)**

Our Father, who art in heaven,
hallowed be thy name;
thy kingdom come,
thy will be done
on earth as it is in heaven.
Give us this day our daily bread,
and forgive us our trespasses,
as we forgive those who trespass against us;
and lead us not into temptation,
but deliver us from evil.
Amen.

Hail Mary, full of grace, the Lord is with thee;
blessed art thou among women,
and blessed is the fruit of thy womb, Jesus.
Holy Mary, Mother of God,
pray for us sinners,
now and at the hour of our death.
Amen.

Glory be to the Father, and to the Son, and to the Holy
Spirit; as it was in the beginning, is now, and ever shall
be, world without end.
Amen.

*(Rise)*

**All sing:**

*Cuius animam gementem,*
*Contristatam et dolentem,*
*Pertransivit gladius.*

Through her heart, his sorrow sharing,
All his bitter anguish bearing,
Now at length the sword had passed.

# *JESUS FALLS*
# *FOR THE FIRST TIME*

℣. We adore you, O Christ, and we bless you. *(Genuflect)*
℟. Because by your holy cross you have redeemed the world. *(Rise)*

**Leader:** Jesus—crowned with thorns and already almost drained of blood—is made to carry his cross. As he makes his painful way to Calvary, bearing the burdens of the world's sin, he falls under the tremendous weight. *(Kneel)*

**All pray:** Lord Jesus, we so often see the universe as turning around our egos and needs. Rescue us from the insanity of sin, which brings about spiritual disintegration and death. As you bore our burdens, disempowering them from within, may we actively lower ourselves to bear the burdens of others.

**(Optional)**

Our Father, who art in heaven,
hallowed be thy name;
thy kingdom come,
thy will be done
on earth as it is in heaven.
Give us this day our daily bread,
and forgive us our trespasses,
as we forgive those who trespass against us;
and lead us not into temptation,
but deliver us from evil.
Amen.

Hail Mary, full of grace, the Lord is with thee;
blessed art thou among women,
and blessed is the fruit of thy womb, Jesus.
Holy Mary, Mother of God,
pray for us sinners,
now and at the hour of our death.
Amen.

Glory be to the Father, and to the Son, and to the Holy
Spirit; as it was in the beginning, is now, and ever shall
be, world without end.
Amen.

*(Rise)*

**All sing:**

*O quam tristis et afflicta*
*Fuit illa benedicta*
*Mater Unigeniti!*

Oh, how sad and sore distressed
Was that Mother highly blest
Of the sole-begotten One!

# *JESUS MEETS HIS BLESSED MOTHER*

℣. We adore you, O Christ, and we bless you.
*(Genuflect)*
℟. Because by your holy cross you have redeemed
the world. *(Rise)*

**Leader:** As he carries the cross, Jesus meets his
Blessed Mother, the Virgin Mary. The humble
handmaid through whom Christ was born now
watches him approach his death, a sword of sorrow
piercing her soul. *(Kneel)*

**All pray:** Holy Mary, you followed your son all the
way to the cross, where he entrusted us to you as
our mother and the privileged channel of his grace.
Intercede for us, that we might be drawn into deeper
fellowship with him.

**(Optional)**

Our Father, who art in heaven,
hallowed be thy name;
thy kingdom come,
thy will be done
on earth as it is in heaven.
Give us this day our daily bread,
and forgive us our trespasses,
as we forgive those who trespass against us;
and lead us not into temptation,
but deliver us from evil.
Amen.

Hail Mary, full of grace, the Lord is with thee;
blessed art thou among women,
and blessed is the fruit of thy womb, Jesus.
Holy Mary, Mother of God,
pray for us sinners,
now and at the hour of our death.
Amen.

Glory be to the Father, and to the Son, and to the Holy
Spirit; as it was in the beginning, is now, and ever shall
be, world without end.
Amen.

*(Rise)*

**All sing:**

*Quae moerebat, et dolebat,*
*Pia Mater, dum videbat*
*Nati poenas inclyti.*

Christ above in torment hangs;
She beneath beholds the pangs
Of her dying glorious Son.

### The Fifth Station
# *SIMON OF CYRENE IS MADE TO HELP JESUS BEAR THE CROSS*

℣. We adore you, O Christ, and we bless you. *(Genuflect)*

℟. Because by your holy cross you have redeemed the world. *(Rise)*

**Leader:** The Romans, not wanting Christ to die before his Crucifixion, press into service Simon of Cyrene. How perilous and dangerous this must have seemed to Simon! But he seizes the moment and helps Jesus with the cross, bearing some of his suffering. *(Kneel)*

**All pray:** Lord Jesus, at the moment of truth, Simon of Cyrene saw that you had need of him—and he responded. Help us, too, to see and respond to your need of us. Even if we are unnoticed or mocked, press us into service to bear you into the world.

**(Optional)**

Our Father, who art in heaven,
hallowed be thy name;
thy kingdom come,
thy will be done
on earth as it is in heaven.
Give us this day our daily bread,
and forgive us our trespasses,
as we forgive those who trespass against us;
and lead us not into temptation,
but deliver us from evil.
Amen.

Hail Mary, full of grace, the Lord is with thee;
blessed art thou among women,
and blessed is the fruit of thy womb, Jesus.
Holy Mary, Mother of God,
pray for us sinners,
now and at the hour of our death.
Amen.

Glory be to the Father, and to the Son, and to the Holy
Spirit; as it was in the beginning, is now, and ever shall
be, world without end.
Amen.

*(Rise)*

**All sing:**

*Quis est homo qui non fleret,*
*Matrem Christi si videret*
*In tanto supplicio?*

Is there one who would not weep,
Whelmed in miserics so deep
Christ's dear Mother to behold?

# The Sixth Station
## *VERONICA WIPES*
## *THE FACE OF JESUS*

℣. We adore you, O Christ, and we bless you. *(Genuflect)*

℟. Because by your holy cross you have redeemed the world. *(Rise)*

**Leader:** A woman called Veronica approaches and wipes the blood and sweat from Jesus' face as he continues his way to Calvary. An image of the face of Christ—the divine Word made flesh—is miraculously imprinted on her veil. *(Kneel)*

**All pray:** Lord Jesus, in your Holy Face, we see the ugliness of our sin, which rules out our self-justification. But we also see the face of mercy, which lifts us from our self-reproach. In your agonies, you reveal our agony and take it away. Keep our gaze fixed on yours, and strengthen us in our mission of drawing the whole world toward you.

**(Optional)**

Our Father, who art in heaven,
hallowed be thy name;
thy kingdom come,
thy will be done
on earth as it is in heaven.
Give us this day our daily bread,
and forgive us our trespasses,
as we forgive those who trespass against us;
and lead us not into temptation,
but deliver us from evil.
Amen.

Hail Mary, full of grace, the Lord is with thee;
blessed art thou among women,
and blessed is the fruit of thy womb, Jesus.
Holy Mary, Mother of God,
pray for us sinners,
now and at the hour of our death.
Amen.

Glory be to the Father, and to the Son, and to the Holy
Spirit; as it was in the beginning, is now, and ever shall
be, world without end.
Amen.

*(Rise)*

**All sing:**

*Quis non posset contristari*
*Christi Matrem contemplari*
*Dolentem cum Filio?*

Can the human heart refrain
From partaking in her pain,
In that Mother's pain untold?

# The Seventh Station
## *JESUS FALLS*
## *FOR THE SECOND TIME*

℣. We adore you, O Christ, and we bless you.
*(Genuflect)*
℟. Because by your holy cross you have redeemed
the world. *(Rise)*

**Leader:** Under the overwhelming weight of the
cross, Jesus falls a second time. Here is the suffering
servant prophesied by Isaiah, who is wounded for
our transgressions and crushed for our iniquities. By
enduring the pain of the cross, he indeed bears our
sins; by his stripes, we are indeed healed. *(Kneel)*

**All pray:** Lord Jesus, you entered into our suffering
and thereby sanctified it. Make us not only willing
to suffer, but willing to suffer as you did, absorbing
violence and hatred through our forgiveness and
nonviolence.

**(Optional)**

Our Father, who art in heaven,
hallowed be thy name;
thy kingdom come,
thy will be done
on earth as it is in heaven.
Give us this day our daily bread,
and forgive us our trespasses,
as we forgive those who trespass against us;
and lead us not into temptation,
but deliver us from evil.
Amen.

Hail Mary, full of grace, the Lord is with thee;
blessed art thou among women,
and blessed is the fruit of thy womb, Jesus.
Holy Mary, Mother of God,
pray for us sinners,
now and at the hour of our death.
Amen.

Glory be to the Father, and to the Son, and to the Holy
Spirit; as it was in the beginning, is now, and ever shall
be, world without end.
Amen.

*(Rise)*

**All sing:**

*Pro peccatis suae gentis*
*Vidit Iesum in tormentis,*
*Et flagellis subditum.*

Bruised, derided, cursed, defiled,
She beheld her tender Child
All with bloody scourges rent.

The Eighth Station
# JESUS MEETS THE
# WOMEN OF JERUSALEM

℣. We adore you, O Christ, and we bless you. *(Genuflect)*
℞. Because by your holy cross you have redeemed the world. *(Rise)*

**Leader:** As Jesus is led to Calvary, a great number follow him, including the weeping women of Jerusalem. Jesus turns to them and speaks as judge of the world, saying, "Daughters of Jerusalem, do not weep for me; weep instead for yourselves and for your children." *(Kneel)*

**All pray:** Lord Jesus, you are the Savior who shows us the way out of our sin. But you are also the Judge who shows us we are sinners. Your every move, word, and gesture, especially your violent death, constituted God's judgment on the world. Whenever we are tempted to think that all is well with us, direct our gaze to your cross, where our illusions die.

**(Optional)**

Our Father, who art in heaven,
hallowed be thy name;
thy kingdom come,
thy will be done
on earth as it is in heaven.
Give us this day our daily bread,
and forgive us our trespasses,
as we forgive those who trespass against us;
and lead us not into temptation,
but deliver us from evil.
Amen.

Hail Mary, full of grace, the Lord is with thee;
blessed art thou among women,
and blessed is the fruit of thy womb, Jesus.
Holy Mary, Mother of God,
pray for us sinners,
now and at the hour of our death.
Amen.

Glory be to the Father, and to the Son, and to the Holy
Spirit; as it was in the beginning, is now, and ever shall
be, world without end.
Amen.

*(Rise)*

**All sing:**

*Vidit suum dulcem Natum*
*Moriendo desolatum,*
*Dum emisit spiritum.*

For the sins of his own nation,
Saw him hang in desolation,
Till his Spirit forth he sent.

## The Ninth Station
## *JESUS FALLS*
## *FOR THE THIRD TIME*

℣. We adore you, O Christ, and we bless you.
*(Genuflect)*
℟. Because by your holy cross you have redeemed the world. *(Rise)*

**Leader:** Jesus continues to bear the terrible weight of the cross—a cross so heavy that it causes him to fall for a third time. Bearing the weight of our sin, and entering into our suffering, Jesus now rises to approach the final enemy to be defeated: death itself. *(Kneel)*

**All pray:** Lord Jesus, at the root of sin is fear, especially fear of death. Thus, you journeyed into the realm of death and, by your sacrifice, twisted it back to life. You conquered death precisely by dying. Keep us from living in a world dominated by death and the fear of death, and help us to remember that death does not have the final word.

**(Optional)**

Our Father, who art in heaven,
hallowed be thy name;
thy kingdom come,
thy will be done
on earth as it is in heaven.
Give us this day our daily bread,
and forgive us our trespasses,
as we forgive those who trespass against us;
and lead us not into temptation,
but deliver us from evil.
Amen.

Hail Mary, full of grace, the Lord is with thee;
blessed art thou among women,
and blessed is the fruit of thy womb, Jesus.
Holy Mary, Mother of God,
pray for us sinners,
now and at the hour of our death.
Amen.

Glory be to the Father, and to the Son, and to the Holy
Spirit; as it was in the beginning, is now, and ever shall
be, world without end.
Amen.

*(Rise)*

**All sing:**

*Eia Mater, fons amoris,*
*Me sentire vim doloris*
*Fac, ut tecum lugeam.*

O thou Mother! fount of love!
Touch my spirit from above,
Make my heart with thine accord.

# JESUS IS STRIPPED
# OF HIS GARMENTS

℣. We adore you, O Christ, and we bless you.
*(Genuflect)*
℟. Because by your holy cross you have redeemed the world. *(Rise)*

**Leader:** The soldiers take Jesus' clothes and divide them into four shares, a share for each soldier, and cast lots for his tunic, fulfilling the words of the Psalm: "They divided my garments among them, and for my vesture they cast lots." Christ is stripped of everything: reputation, comfort, esteem, food, drink—even the pathetic clothes on his back. *(Kneel)*

**All pray:** Lord Jesus, on the way of the cross, you despised the addictions of wealth, pleasure, power, and honor, and you loved the will of your Father. You were stripped naked, utterly detached from worldly goods. You went into the furthest reaches of godforsakenness in order to bring the divine love even to that darkest place. Grant that we may despise what you despised, and love what you loved.

**(Optional)**

Our Father, who art in heaven,
hallowed be thy name;
thy kingdom come,
thy will be done
on earth as it is in heaven.
Give us this day our daily bread,
and forgive us our trespasses,
as we forgive those who trespass against us;
and lead us not into temptation,
but deliver us from evil.
Amen.

Hail Mary, full of grace, the Lord is with thee;
blessed art thou among women,
and blessed is the fruit of thy womb, Jesus.
Holy Mary, Mother of God,
pray for us sinners,
now and at the hour of our death.
Amen.

Glory be to the Father, and to the Son, and to the Holy
Spirit; as it was in the beginning, is now, and ever shall
be, world without end.
Amen.

*(Rise)*

**All sing:**

*Fac, ut ardeat cor meum*
*In amando Christum Deum*
*Ut sibi complaceam.*

Make me feel as thou hast felt;
Make my soul to glow and melt
With the love of Christ my Lord.

# The Eleventh Station
## *JESUS IS CRUCIFIED*

℣. We adore you, O Christ, and we bless you.
*(Genuflect)*
℞. Because by your holy cross you have redeemed
the world. *(Rise)*

**Leader:** Jesus is crucified between two criminals,
saying, "Father, forgive them, they know not
what they do." Dying on a Roman instrument of
torture, undergoing excruciating pain, he allows
the full force of the world's hatred and dysfunction
to wash over him, to spend itself on him. And he
responds not with violence or resentment but with
forgiveness. *(Kneel)*

**All pray:** Lord Jesus, in your Crucifixion, you took
away the sin of the world, swallowing it up in the
divine mercy. Through your perfect sacrifice as high
priest, eternal life has been made available to the
whole of humanity. Stir up your Church to deepen
its participation in this eternal act through the
Mass, where we unite our sacrifices with yours.

**(Optional)**

Our Father, who art in heaven,
hallowed be thy name;
thy kingdom come,
thy will be done
on earth as it is in heaven.
Give us this day our daily bread,
and forgive us our trespasses,
as we forgive those who trespass against us;
and lead us not into temptation,
but deliver us from evil.
Amen.

Hail Mary, full of grace, the Lord is with thee;
blessed art thou among women,
and blessed is the fruit of thy womb, Jesus.
Holy Mary, Mother of God,
pray for us sinners,
now and at the hour of our death.
Amen.

Glory be to the Father, and to the Son, and to the Holy
Spirit; as it was in the beginning, is now, and ever shall
be, world without end.
Amen.

*(Rise)*

**All sing:**

*Sancta Mater, istud agas,*
*Crucifixi fige plagas*
*Cordi meo valide.*

Holy Mother! pierce me through;
In my heart each wound renew
Of my Savior crucified.

## The Twelfth Station
## *JESUS DIES ON THE CROSS*

℣. We adore you, O Christ, and we bless you. *(Genuflect)*
℟. Because by your holy cross you have redeemed the world. *(Rise)*

**Leader:** From the cross, Jesus says "Consummatum est"—"It is finished." The work of the Lord has been brought to fulfillment. He gives out a loud cry, and breathes his last. Above the crucified God hangs a sign placed by Pontius Pilate and written out in Hebrew, Greek, and Latin: "Jesus the Nazorean, the King of the Jews." *(Kneel)*

**All pray:** Lord Jesus, you are the new David, the one who fulfills salvation history and finally rescues humanity. Help us to announce the message that Pilate first announced unwittingly, the message that every person was born to hear: that you are the new King.

**(Optional)**

Our Father, who art in heaven,
hallowed be thy name;
thy kingdom come,
thy will be done
on earth as it is in heaven.
Give us this day our daily bread,
and forgive us our trespasses,
as we forgive those who trespass against us;
and lead us not into temptation,
but deliver us from evil.
Amen.

Hail Mary, full of grace, the Lord is with thee;
blessed art thou among women,
and blessed is the fruit of thy womb, Jesus.
Holy Mary, Mother of God,
pray for us sinners,
now and at the hour of our death.
Amen.

Glory be to the Father, and to the Son, and to the Holy
Spirit; as it was in the beginning, is now, and ever shall
be, world without end.
Amen.

*(Rise)*

**All sing:**

*Tui Nati vulnerati,*
*Tam dignati pro me pati,*
*Poenas mecum divide.*

Let me share with thee his pain,
Who for all my sins was slain,
Who for me in torments died.

# *JESUS IS TAKEN DOWN FROM THE CROSS AND LAID IN THE ARMS OF MARY*

℣. We adore you, O Christ, and we bless you. *(Genuflect)*
℟. Because by your holy cross you have redeemed the world. *(Rise)*

**Leader:** After the Crucifixion, Jesus is taken from the cross and laid in the arms of Mary, the definitive Ark of the Covenant, who carried the incarnate Word in her very womb. At his birth, Mary placed Jesus in a manger, where animals eat. Now, at his death, she presents him as food for the life of the world. *(Kneel)*

**All pray:** Lord Jesus, the Blessed Virgin Mary cradled you in her arms. Marked with your blood, she presented your sacrifice to us and for us. In her offering of your body, may we be reminded of the Church's continual offering of your Body in the Eucharist.

**(Optional)**

Our Father, who art in heaven,
hallowed be thy name;
thy kingdom come,
thy will be done
on earth as it is in heaven.
Give us this day our daily bread,
and forgive us our trespasses,
as we forgive those who trespass against us;
and lead us not into temptation,
but deliver us from evil.
Amen.

Hail Mary, full of grace, the Lord is with thee;
blessed art thou among women,
and blessed is the fruit of thy womb, Jesus.
Holy Mary, Mother of God,
pray for us sinners,
now and at the hour of our death.
Amen.

Glory be to the Father, and to the Son, and to the Holy
Spirit; as it was in the beginning, is now, and ever shall
be, world without end.
Amen.

*(Rise)*

**All sing:**

*Fac me tecum pie flere,*
*Crucifixo condolere,*
*Donec ego vixero.*

Let me mingle tears with thee,
Mourning him who mourned for me,
All the days that I may live.

# *JESUS IS LAID IN THE TOMB*

℣. We adore you, O Christ, and we bless you.
*(Genuflect)*
℟. Because by your holy cross you have redeemed the world. *(Rise)*

**Leader:** Joseph of Arimathea, a secret admirer of Jesus, comes courageously to ask for the body of the Lord, and a group of women who had accompanied Jesus from Galilee watch carefully to see where he is buried. His enemies had closed in on him, and most of his intimate friends had fled in fear, but these faithful disciples stay with Jesus until the end. *(Kneel)*

**All pray:** Lord Jesus, make our discipleship as complete and consistent as the women who followed you from Galilee to the grave. You went to the cross because you love your Father's will; let we who love you go to that same bitter end, knowing that the stone of our resting place will, like yours, be one day rolled away. Fill our hearts with the joy of the empty tomb, and make us bold in sharing the Good News of your Resurrection.

**(Optional)**

Our Father, who art in heaven,
hallowed be thy name;
thy kingdom come,
thy will be done
on earth as it is in heaven.
Give us this day our daily bread,
and forgive us our trespasses,
as we forgive those who trespass against us;
and lead us not into temptation,
but deliver us from evil.
Amen.

Hail Mary, full of grace, the Lord is with thee;
blessed art thou among women,
and blessed is the fruit of thy womb, Jesus.
Holy Mary, Mother of God,
pray for us sinners,
now and at the hour of our death.
Amen.

Glory be to the Father, and to the Son, and to the Holy
Spirit; as it was in the beginning, is now, and ever shall
be, world without end.
Amen.

*(Rise)*

**All sing:**

*Iuxta Crucem tecum stare,*
*Et me tibi sociare*
*In planctu desidero.*

By the cross with thee to stay;
There with thee to weep and pray;
Is all I ask of thee to give.

# *CLOSING PRAYER*

**From St. Thérèse of Lisieux's Act of Oblation to Merciful Love**

**All pray:** I thank you, O my God, for all the graces you have granted me, especially the grace of making me pass through the crucible of suffering. It is with joy I shall contemplate you on the Last Day carrying the scepter of your cross. Since you deigned to give me a share in this very precious cross, I hope in heaven to resemble you and to see shining in my glorified body the sacred stigmata of your Passion.
Amen.

In the name of the Father, and of the Son, and of the Holy Spirit.
Amen.

# Do you wish you had a book with daily meditations and Scripture passages you could use beyond Lent?

The Liturgy of the Hours is the official prayer of the Church. It is an ancient, structured way of praying that focuses on the Psalms and helps us make Christ the center of every day.

Get started today at **wordonfire.org/pray**